GREG ASHLEY'S

ANECDOTES

Albums by Greg Ashley

THE MIRRORS – A GREEN DREAM

THE MIRRORS – 13 PATIENT FLOWERS

GREG ASHLEY – MEDICINE FUCK DREAM

THE GRIS GRIS

GRIS GRIS – FOR THE SEASON

GRIS GRIS – LIVE AT THE CREAMERY

GREG ASHLEY – PAINTED GARDEN

GREG ASHLEY – REQUIEM MASS & OTHER
EXPERIMENTS

GREG ASHLEY'S – DEATH OF A LADIES' MAN

GREG ASHLEY – ANOTHER GENERATION OF
SLAVES

GREG ASHLEY – & THE WESTERN PLAYBOYS

GREG ASHLEY – PICTURES OF SAINT PAUL
STREET

GREG ASHLEY – FICTION IS NON-FICTION

The gutter is a fine place to start, but it's a shit place to end up.

-Billy Childish

Contents

-THE DEATH OF KAREN COLLINS-

I woke up that morning in Echo Park in a blond girl's bed. I was naked. I was on my way to Houston. My phone rang, it was Karen's sister Megan, "Greg, Karen's dead.........she's dead." Megan is bawling, I don't know what to make of this. How could Karen be dead? We were all in our early 20's. I wasn't expecting any of my friends to die anytime soon, especially not Karen. I thought maybe Megan was trying to get one over on me. She liked to mess with people's heads. I liked her, she was mischievous and wild. I guess we all were, all the League City crew.

I say to her, "Megan, shut up. Why are you calling me with this bullshit at 8 in the morning? Fuck you." I hang up. I call Sam, he tells me Karen died last night. I call Megan back and apologize. I suppose we talked for a bit and then the call ended.

Karen had died from from a heroin overdose. She was naturally thin and didn't use heroin, at least not on a regular basis. I guess her body just couldn't handle it. Her and Catalina got drunk, snorted some heroin and then passed out. Catalina woke up next to her. That really did a number on her. I can't imagine waking up next to your best friend like that. Fucking terrible.

I grew up with both of them. I'd known Catalina since the 7th grade. I met Karen in the summer of 1999. They had both moved to New York City after high school. Well, Catalina moved right after high school to start her studies at Columbia. Karen moved a few years later and was taking photography classes at City College there.

After the call I was in total shock. I was just numb the whole day. Me and my new LA friends, Carolyn and Kyle, went to a party that evening. There were fireworks at midnight. I blacked out and woke up on a strange couch the next morning. From then on, the 4th of July fireworks would mean something entirely different for me.

The next day, I picked up a dog I was hired on Craigslist to drive from LA to Austin. It was an old dog, big black thing, a black lab. The air conditioning in my Honda was busted as well as the transmission. Me and this dog had to drive across over a thousand miles of desert in July with no AC and if you tried to speed up in a way that made the car down-shift, it slipped into the clutch and you had to throw it in neutral and pull over. I'd have to come to a complete stop and then start over. It shifted up just fine. Down, not so much. So no passing anything fast and any change in the grade of the road upward meant I just had to go slower and slower and slower until I came to a complete stop.......

It was over a hundred degrees in the California and Arizona deserts and I was pouring water on this poor old black furry dog all day long. If I remember correctly, me and the dog got from Los Angeles to Van Horn, TX in one long day. We stayed in a twenty dollar motel room with a five dollar fee for the dog. After a long day of driving and being stuck in my head with no-one to talk to, I wanted nothing more than to get drunk. I had wine but no corkscrew, so I threw a bottle of Charles Shaw into the microwave until the pressure started to shift the cork slowly up the neck of the bottle. When it was far enough out I took the bottle out of the microwave and got my teeth

2

around the cork. The wine was warm and kind of gross, but I drank it anyways and passed out.

The next day we drove on to Austin. I still hadn't been able to process Karen's death. I called Lisa, my girlfriend at the time, and told her Karen was dead. She was surprised I hadn't said anything sooner. I called my family. There response was, "Suicide?"

"No" I said. I dropped the dog in Austin. I think I probably stayed in Austin that night, but I don't remember where or with whom. Probably Sam.

I got to the Houston area the next day and I don't think I even stopped at my parents place in League City. I think I just drove straight to Karen's dad's house in Nassau Bay to see Phil (Karen's dad) and Megan. Chad was living there at the time, and yes, her dad's name is Phil Collins. I don't know if the body had been delivered from New York yet but they had her underwear in a ziplock bag for some reason. I remember I was going to open up the bag and Chad said, "Don't open that dude." So I didn't.

I think that's when it set in. I think that might have been when I first started to cry. I went to my folks place. I remember my mom saying they would be there for me at the funeral. I told them not to come. I love my parents, but I didn't wanna be uncomfortable at the funeral. My relationship with my family has always been a little strange. We are not estranged, but my parents and my sister are just completely different kinds of people than me. All the things they frowned upon were the things that made me smile. Drug use, promiscuity, vulgarity, what I thought of as the spice of life.

Much of our not seeing eye to eye was due, at least in

part to the fact that my parents are from a distant generation. They were born in 1940 and 1941, before the baby boom. Thank God my parents weren't a couple of self-righteous hippies, but at least let me smoke a joint and get a piece Mom and Dad. They're pretty much squares is what they are. Free thinkers for sure, but squares none the less. They're open minded and smart, and they've adjusted their views, when necessary, to accept some of my indiscretions over the years. But back then things were still fairly uncomfortable for me. I had zero appreciation for the example they had set of how to live a good and decent life. My mom taught me how to read, write, and do arithmetic before I even started school. They were great parents.

Anyways, I remember going to the funeral home on Main Street in League City. They let me view the body privately before the service. I was led into the room with the casket and there she was. Embalmed I suppose. They buried her in jeans and a t-shirt, just like she always dressed. I remember her dad saying he wanted it that way. He liked the way she was so understated and wanted to remember her the way she actually was. I stayed there for a long time just sitting with her crying.

The service was the next day. I got to the funeral home early to be with her again. I remember meeting her aunt that she was named after. Then all our friends started to arrive. Catalina showed up with a flask. We sat and drank liquor in the back of my mom's old van and talked. She was ruined. She had so much guilt. All the old League City crew showed up. Roadhouse, Tom, Chad, Alan, Trey, almost all my old high school friends, and The Boylands

4

too of course: Rachel, Shana, Carla and Phil. I'd never seen Phil Boyland cry. He was such a tough bastard, but he cried that day. Just like the rest of us. "Poor sweet Karen," he said. And he was right.

Me and Catalina sat in the front, on the right side of the Chapel. Karen's family was on the left. It was just me and her on the pew. We went up to the casket for the viewing and I kissed my hand and touched it to Karen's forehead. It moved in a strange lifeless way that shocked me. I remember everyone was sobbing, men and women alike. I went over to her dad and he says to me, "Get me John." I thought he was talking about John Johnson so I grabbed him. Wrong John. He was asking about the John that Karen had been dating at the time. I'd forgotten about him. Her dad kept saying he didn't want them to close the casket. He said, "When they close that casket I'm never going to see her again." That was true, none of us ever saw Karen again. Mom and Dad and Sister all gave eulogies. I don't know how they did it. I couldn't speak, and wasn't asked to.

The wake was that evening. Everyone from the old days was there, and we all got shit-faced. My memory of this is, of course, pretty spotty. I remember sitting on the roof of the garage to Karen's house drinking whiskey with Chad and Sam, talking about death and what the possibilities were. Too bad for us, we all agreed you just go in the ground and rot. I remember a conversation with Karen's dad about some pretty strange things, no details though. We were all out of our minds. Everyone in shock, just crying and laughing and falling over drunk. Total chaos.

Megan had Karen's cell phone. If a call was missed on the phone you got a computer message. If a call was rejected on the phone you would hear Karen's voice. "Hi, this is Karen, leave a message." It was good to hear her voice. I sat there and made Megan reject my calls over and over again. "Do it again." I would say. "Again." That was the last time I would hear her voice.

The service was held at the Jack Roe Funeral Home in League City. Karen was to be buried in Austin. So the next day Me, Catalina, Chad, Alan, and Larry (Catalina's sort of boyfriend) all piled into my mom's old minivan and headed for Austin. We got to the graveyard, they put her coffin in the ground, and gave me and Catalina and Karen's family each a rose. I kept mine in my guitar case until it fell apart and then fell out of the case. Catalina threw hers on the coffin. She said she wanted Karen to have it. Then we each put a shovel of dirt on the grave.

When I think of all the twists and turns my life has taken since then, I can't organize any of it at all. It's just a blur of missteps, mistakes, and generally shit behavior. I wouldn't change any of it. I guess it's part of growing up. I wish there was something I could have done to change this though. I think if she'd been around the last 13 years things would have been different. She's missing the middle and the end. Things are starting to unfold. It starts to look like that more and more every day. I think all the lines would have been more defined had she been around. No, actually they wouldn't have been. Everything would be just as fucked as it is today. Just, she would have been here for it.

I used to go to her grave every time I went to Austin. It took years for her family to get the headstone, but I memorized where she was buried and would go to her grave, stone or not. Eventually it was laid on the grave. A flat stone. It reads, "Karen Collins Jan 29, 1982 - July 3, 2005" and then a line from a song I wrote. Catalina died on July 7th, 2013. She jumped out the window of her third floor apartment in Harlem. She never got over Karen's death. I'll never get over either of them.

-MY DOCTOR, ALCOHOLICS ANONYMOUS, GOD & DMT-

Let me tell you about my doctor. We'll just call her "The Ballerina", because she used to be one. She is a flirtatious, pill dispensing bundle of joy. I actually like going to the doctor, at least when I'm pretty much well. Going to any doctor when you need to be detoxed from alcohol is painful as well as painfully embarrassing. I've been to her three times for this. The Ballerina is never judgmental, she just writes me an RX for the meds we both know I need and says, "Take these meds, and I want you to come see me everyday for a week. It's Thursday, and the clinic is closed over the weekend, so continue to drink until Sunday. On Sunday start taking the withdrawal pills and I'll see you on Monday." No problem doc, I can surely keep boozing through the weekend if that's what it's gonna take.

She flirts with me less after this. But that only lasts until the follow-up, after that it's back to, "Why don't you come see me more often? I never see you anymore." I went today, it was great. I needed different sleeping pills. The ones I was using stopped working, they always do. Trazadone, great. After a month or so, not only are they ineffective, but they start giving me nightmares. Seroquel, worked for a few months then not so much. Ambien, same, also weird dreams, now I'm back to Seroquel. I have fallen off the wagon a dozen times just because I couldn't fucking sleep. Nothing is worse than insomnia, I've had it my whole life.

I've been going to a lot of AA meetings for the last few

months. Not because I want to, but because I have been court ordered to. I got a DUI this last summer. I made the fatal mistake of driving 20 feet into Emeryville to park my truck when I drove to the liquor store at quarter to 2AM after a gig. I got pulled over leaving the store, made an illegal U-turn. Didn't help my situation either that I was three times over the legal limit and in possession of a crack pipe and two bars of Xanax.

I spent the night in jail, the pigs took my blood and I was out in the morning minus my license. I flipped out and started drinking even more. I was supposed to go to Canada in a couple weeks to see this girl I had been dating in Vancouver. I had to cancel that trip. I haven't seen her in five months now. Don't know when I'll be able, if ever, to enter Canada again. They are pretty hard-core about not admitting people into their country that have a drunk driving record. There is supposedly some class you can take and fees you can pay to make entry into Canada a possibility again. This is apparently thanks to George W. Bush. He has something like three DUIs on his record. When he became the leader of the free world back at the beginning of the millennium, Canada had to soften its zero tolerance policy on drunk driving. They couldn't have the president of The United States not able to enter their country now could they? (This whole George W. Bush bit could be total bullshit for all I know. That's just what I heard.) I haven't looked into those classes yet, because I don't have a pot to piss in, and I'm still waiting to hear what my fines will be from Alameda County.

Anyways, part of my "bail" is to attend at least one AA meeting a week until the final verdict is laid down in my case. I've had two court dates so far where I show up, don't say shit, and my lawyer schmoozes with the DA and says some bullshit to the judge. Each time they set another court date and my lawyer assures me, "I'm buying us some more time. I'm gonna put some pressure on these guys." I don't know how this is possible, but we'll see if I get my $2,500 dollars worth out of this sleazy motherfucker.

I've watched while the poor bastards on trial with a public defender get fucked by the legal system over and over again. I'm thinkin', "Pressure? Are we gonna bribe these people? Let's fucking do it." He told me to go to two AA meetings a week, so I have tried to go to as many as I can possibly make myself. I have gone everyday except for one for the last three weeks, including the day of our last court date. I missed one because I got in an accident on my bike. Broke two of my teeth in half and had a scab that ran down my face for three weeks. I could barely eat. I'm going to so many meetings because I've heard that it can help decrease the amount of DUI school you have to attend, and possibly lighten your sentence. I need all the help I can get I figure.

AA usually drives me nuts. The idea of it is all good and well, but the whole program is structured around accepting that there is a god, or higher power of some sort, that you have to surrender to in order to quit drinking. It works for a bunch of people and more power to them. If magic helps you quit drinking, great! Drinking has royally fucked up my life and destroyed many a relationship and opportunity for me. That being said, I'm not gonna start believing in nonsense and fairy tales. Although I will go along with the first of the twelve steps and admit that I'm powerless over alcohol. I certainly can't drink at all anymore. I've tried moderation and it doesn't work for me. That doesn't mean there's a god though.

Modern medicine has found that people like me have a defect in their brain that makes us more susceptible to alcohol addiction. No magic there, just defective. For some people it's cocaine or heroin. For me it's booze. I've done heroin, makes me sick. Some people it doesn't. I know some of them. They became junkies. Not their fault, if junk didn't make me puke nine times out of ten I'd probably be a junky and an alcoholic. Cocaine makes me really nervous and edgy. Some people it relaxes them. I only like coke when I'm drunk, and that's just so I can drink more.

God and religion exist in human societies primarily to explain the things that human beings cannot explain. Where did we come from? What does it all mean? Why does the sun rise and fall? What are the stars? Why do they move around the sky the way they do?

Now science has obviously answered many of the questions that religion grappled with in the past. We now have the theory of evolution and know the earth turns on an axis and orbits the sun. And the stars are other suns, in distant solar systems, millions of light years away, all shooting through the expanse of space. Whatever space is....... We call dark matter and dark energy what we do because we don't know what they are. Either way, educated people no longer use religion to answer questions of the unknown. So why the fuck am I gonna use a book written by two middle class white guys in 1938, who believe in magic, to solve my drinking problem?

There are experiences I have had in my life that I cannot explain. One of the most riveting was a DMT trip I took back in 2017. Me and Jess took MDMA at the church. After we were rolling we smoked DMT out of a glass pipe we bought at a head shop. This is the only effective way to break through on DMT. I've only gotten there once and this is what happened.

I'm sitting on my bed. I fill the bulb of the glass pipe with a bunch of the yellow DMT powder that smells like moth balls. I take as many hits as I can, as quickly as I can, and then boom! My vision goes black. I no longer hear whatever record we had been listening to. I come to in an observation room made of glowing florescent tiles. There is a table in the middle of the room made of these tiles and there are two short alien creatures next to the table. Their heads are like the heads of a joker in a deck of cards. I'm totally comfortable, not scared at all. Me and the harlequins (that's what other people refer to them as) don't speak to one and other. We just hang out. Fuckin' nuts. Eventually a panel slides out from the wall and the harlequins motion for me to lie down on the panel. I'm cool with all this, but I decide I'm not lying down on that fucking panel, that's just past my threshold. I open my eyes. I'm back in the church, Jess is holding me, looking into my eyes and asking me if everything is alright. She looks like she has a green sheet of plastic wrapped around her face and body. The whole room kind of has a gelatinous quality to it. I close my eyes and I'm back on the alien space ship, harlequins and all. I hang there for a while then back to the church. I could go back and forth for I think around ten or fifteen minutes, not sure how long.

Anyways, how do I explain that shit? Did I step into another dimension? An alternate reality? It was for sure an out of body experience. I might chalk it up to a simple hallucination if it wasn't for the fact that so many other people I've spoken to have had a shared experience with DMT.

I've also had out of body experiences on really good Ketamine. I snorted that shit and all of a sudden I was no longer trapped in my human form and it's consciousness. I was just pure energy shooting through tubes of space and time.

I've lost my identity on mushrooms, completely forgot who I was. The mushrooms and Ketamine I suppose I could also chalk up to hallucinations, but really what I think these psychedelic drugs are doing is changing my perception of reality. Your perception and what you think of as real is really just a construct of the society in which you live, and the language you use to organize the things you perceive with your senses. Human beings in other parts of the world such as the Amazon, for instance, perceive reality in a drastically different way than we do in the "civilized world". If you dropped some tribesman that's never been out of the jungle in the middle of Tokyo, he wouldn't see a bunch of steel buildings and Asian people. Who knows what the fuck he would see. He would have no way to describe it, to organize it into a place or thing that was recognizable. It would be nonsense to him. Like if we took the raw binary code that is running the word processor I'm writing this on, and tried to read it instead of what the program is spitting out at us in the form of English. 000011 010010101 01010101010. Read that, I didn't. With this computer code running in the background, I'm able to write these words down, and you are able to understand the ideas I'm conveying to you through them. This is because of our shared language, shared experience, and a firm agreement on what these words are and what they represent. And that might seem like magic too, but that doesn't make it so.

I think the constraints of my learned perception were momentarily stripped away and I possibly saw something that was there all along but just couldn't see. Because I am operating on an organization of perception that is discarding certain information deemed irrelevant to my survival as a human. Or I was just fucking high, but either way I'm not gonna go around saying I saw God or extra-terrestrials, because I don't know what I saw. Doesn't mean there's a higher power. Just means, news flash, people don't know everything. I think accepting that is really the break-through that could benefit humankind and the planet. Not blindly following religion which can be twisted and manipulated to control people to act in terrible ways, not to mention, acting against their own self interests and the interest of the planet and the human race as a whole.

Anyways, back to AA. I go to these morning meditation meetings now. They are the only ones I've found that I think are actually helpful and that I can stand to sit through for an hour without wanting to rip what's left of my hair out. There's no reading from an irrelevant out-dated book, not a lot of God bullshit and not a lot of dip-shits blabbing about nothing. The meeting is at 7:40 AM everyday, so it's usually me and a bunch of senior citizens. The meeting starts, you say the AA prayer, then the prayer of Saint Francis, and then you sit in silence for 30 minutes. Great, easy way to get my paper signed for the court every day. And meditation is good for me every morning. Most of the time I'm not really effectively meditating, but a long moment of silence seems to do me some good nonetheless.

The last half of the meeting is free group therapy essentially. This is the last half of most AA meetings. Most other meetings, the first half consists of reading dumb shit out of the old book or listening to a speaker talk about their decent into a life of debauchery and self destruction to eventually rise like a phoenix from the ashes and appear before all of the good people behind these doors to share their experience and possibly shed some light on our common affliction. This is great if the speaker is good, but that shit is hit or miss. I've heard some great ones, and then I've heard some real stupid self absorbed motherfuckers blab nonsense for 30 minutes. I've seen a couple black dudes who all of a sudden think they are baptist ministers and ex-hippies brag about how they knew Mick Jagger, while they pat themselves on the back for their activism back in the dark ages. Look in the mirror grandpa- you sold out. Fuck you, go back to your hole in Berkeley. Silence serves me better obviously.

One morning I spoke a bit during the sharing portion. At the end of the meeting the guy heading the thing thanked me for "my share" and then forced me to give him my phone number saying he sponsors guys. I have no interest in having a sponsor and going through the 12 steps. The meditation and free group therapy is working fine for me. I don't need to muck it up with any of that bullshit. This guy has my number now. He will bother me from here on out. I've had other people get my number before. It fucking sucks. They call you constantly. "I didn't see you at the meeting yesterday. Is everything OK?" I know they mean well, but I have a few friends left. I have a family that loves me, even if my mom drives me crazy, and I also have a driving force in my life. Something to strive towards other than just getting fucked up all the time to get through my horrible meaningless existence.

I went to AA yesterday and met with my sponsor afterwards. Turns out he's an OK dude. Maybe I'll give this thing a shot, or stop going after my last court appearance..........yeah I stopped going.

-CLEAR CREEK HIGH SCHOOL-

The high school we all went to was a fucking joke, or most of us just didn't bother to apply ourselves or show up for that matter. My parents sent me to private school in 4th and 5th grade. I went back to public school in 6th grade. I wanted to go back. My parents were cheap, and they went to public school so why not me. I quickly learned to fit in and play dumb. I made friends with all the other outcasts and weirdos on the fringe at my school. I learned to drink and smoke pot. I learned to fuck, eventually. I had poor friends, rich friends, white, yellow, black, and brown friends. I had friends that were fat, skinny, short, and tall.

I was pretty much a year ahead when I got back to public school, and it continued to seem that way until I graduated. Probably due to the fact that in high school I took only the bare minimum and easiest of classes required to graduate. I hated school, at least the part when I was in class. I had plenty of time to fuck off, and fuck off I did.

I skipped school as much as I could get away with. My freshman year the two most frequent locations for this activity would have been either John and Chrissie's place or Hutch's place. Kids who had only one parent around or two working parents always had the spot. And if their folks were rich, like John and Chrissie's, even better. They had a pool, a pool table, their parent's booze, and marijuana on hand at all times. I had some good times over there getting twisted in the mid-morning/early-afternoon, then stumbling back onto campus to complete my school day.

Our high school had an automated phone system that would call your house in the evening if you missed a class. "Hello this is Clear Creek High School calling to inform you that your son or daughter has missed one or more classes today. If you are unaware of this absence please call us at 554-...."

High school got out at 2:30, the call always came between 4 and 5pm. I'd sit by the phone upstairs in my parents house everyday I skipped class and try to catch that call before someone else did. Some of my friends that were a bit more savvy about the inner workings of the phone system in the late 90s had a much more final and effective approach to making sure their parents never received any of these calls. This is what they did: If you got the call and hung up on it right away the system would call back immediately from another one of the school's phone lines. So they would get the call and continually hang up on it until the school ran out of numbers to call from. Then they would check the caller ID box, write down all the numbers the automated system had called from and block all those numbers. Genius! I don't know why I never did this. Pure laziness I suppose, even though it was a lot more work to catch that fucking call every other day.

Sophomore year I get my license and the first of many hand-me-down cars from my parents. Now I can skip school whenever and where ever I want. I go to Roadhouse's sometimes, he dropped out a few months into sophomore year, but I soon gave up on that cuz he always slept until at least 2 or 3 in the afternoon.

Rachel and Shana's was always an option. During this

time I gave Trevor a ride to school everyday. Trevor was one of my close friends, a great dude. Most mornings I would roll a joint for the ride to school. Me and Trevor would smoke and inevitably he'd ask me, "Man you really wanna go to first period?"

Me, "No, not really."

Trevor, "Let's see what Shana's doing."

Shana was in 8th grade, so she went to middle school, which started at 9am. High school started at 7:30. We'd go to her house, smoke pot with her, take her to middle school, go back to her house, then hang out until we decided to drag ourselves to class.

One day we were watching *Sanford and Son* at her house in the late morning. The phone rings. We don't answer of course. The machine picks up and we hear dialing. We don't talk but the TV's on. We didn't know it, but Carla (Shana's mom) had this answering machine where you could dial a code when it picked up and the internal mic was activated so you could hear what was going on in your house. She calls, hears the TV, calls later, we are gone. She assumes Shana is skipping school. Carla calls the middle school, Shana is in class. She calls the high school, Rachel (Shana's sister) is in class. I don't know what conclusion she ever came to, but it was pretty obvious that all of us were up to no good a large percentage of the time.

My Junior year, the whole like eight person crew of punk kids from League City Intermediate entered high school. The older kids like Josh, Bob, Trevor, Phil, were out, and the young kids were in; Dom, Graham, Alan, Chad, Trey and Shana.

Dom was a good friend, he dated Shana. Dom's mom was a lesbian. She was also a school teacher and I remember her always being paranoid of somebody spilling the beans about her sexuality. And for good reason, she could have lost her job. It was Texas in the late 90's. She wasn't exactly rolling around incognito or anything though. She drove a purple jeep with a rainbow decal on the back hatch and an indigo girls sticker on the bumper. That flare spoke one word to anybody with any sort of gaydar to speak of........... Lesbian.

His parents were divorced but they had an arrangement to keep the family together. Dom's mom and her girlfriend had the master bedroom. Dom's dad had a regular room just like the kids. He had an auto shop for BMWs I think. He also raced dragsters too. A real man's man. He dated his ex-wife's sister for a short time until she too became a lesbian. His dad always seemed a little pissed off but harmless.

Me and Dom's mom got along good. We'd sit out back by the pool, chain smoking Marlboros and gossiping about bullshit. Or his mom would, mostly I just listened. Dom's mother's love for me would turn to hate though somewhere in my senior year of high school.

One night Dom, Graham, and Roadhouse stayed over at my place. We stayed up all night smoking weed, drinking beers and playing video games. I was living in a building in my backyard referred to as "The Garden House", because my mom stored her gardening tools in there. That was my first escape from living under my parent's roof. I could smoke in there, come and go as I pleased without getting harassed, and I even got laid now and then. Around 4am I get the brilliant idea to go down to the Kroger's in Dickinson and steal more beer. Dom comes with me. I'm so drunk I have to close one eye to turn the six lane highway back into a three laner. We enter the grocery store and head for the beer isle. Dom's dumb ass tries to put a whole six pack under his shirt. I crotch a few beers and we head for the door. I'm walking just a little bit ahead of Dom cuz I'm not totally convinced he's getting away with what he's attempting here. And he doesn't, but I do. I sit in the car for five minutes or so trying to figure out what I should do next. An employee comes out the front entrance and stares at me in my car. I drive off - *Fuck this, I'm going home*. I get home, slam a beer and pass out. I'm woken up by my parents around six that morning.

Mom, "Gregory, Gregory wake up. Dom's mother is here, what is going on?"

I'm still drunk, of course, so I get up and play dumb. When I walk into my parents house Dom's mother is there and she starts screaming at me right off the bat. "You left him there, you just left him there!" She starts punching me, no-one stops her including me. But what was I supposed to do? Stay at the grocery store and get arrested too? What good would have that done anybody? That blew over eventually and life returned to whatever normal was. Our poor fucking parents. Dom's mom Facebook messages me every once in a while. I'd like to think we're still friends. Yeah we're still friends, Facebook told me so........

There was Graham. He lived in Baycliff. He went to school now and then but really spent most of his time smoking bud and playing Nintendo 64 in the broken down camper his parent's parked in the front yard. His dad lived in the Philippines for most of his high school years doing some kind of petroleum work out there. His old man ran off with some Filipino chick his sophomore year.

His mom worked for an oil refinery, I think. She'd work ten twelve hour days and then be off for ten. Ten on, ten off, I think it was called. I could be getting this completely wrong but who cares. Either way she'd be around a bunch and then not at all. His house was on about an acre of land. Sometimes you'd see his mom on the riding mower in her bikini, not a pretty sight.

We used to huff freon a lot at Graham's house. So much so that the air conditioning repair guy had to come out and re-charge the AC unit on multiple occasions. The repair guy and Graham's mom figured it was a leak somewhere, but they never found it. I remember Graham's mom coming into the kitchen once when we were preparing a plastic grocery bag to be huffed out of. She walked into the room and Graham just freaked and shoved the bag into a drawer. She came over to look at what he'd put in the drawer and she was dumbfounded. "What the hell are these boys up to now?" She just looked at all of us cockeyed and walked out of the room.

Alan was the son of a Webster cop. His dad was a stern bastard. This one night Alan showed up late for practice and we all gave him shit until he told us what had happened. Alan had been helping his dad move a mattress into the attic of their house. He slipped and put his foot right through the ceiling. This pisses off his dad so much that he punches him in the chest knocking the wind out of him.

In south Texas your attic is not a place you hang out in.

It's fucking hot up there all the time. Most attics are just unfinished, oddly shaped rooms. You have to stand on spaced out 2'x4's with nothing between them but insulation on top of drywall, which was also the ceiling for the room beneath you. The attic would usually have a small standing area at the top of a ladder. Just a piece of plywood laid flat. That was it.

Alan loved to drink, just like the rest of us. I remember doing beer bongs at this guy Jesse's trailer in Old League City. When Alan did his somebody pulled out a flask and loaded up his bong mid slam. Didn't seem to phase him. Later I was driving Alan and some other people home from the party and Alan didn't wanna go home. He was too fucked up. I had to go home. I had an eleven o'clock curfew. He asked me to drive around his neighborhood in circles while he sobered up. Mind you, I'm drunk too. I wanna do as little driving as possible, and I need to get home. Finally I get tired of this and tell him I'm dropping him off.

Alan, "You're such an asshole Greg. All you care about is yourself." Then he starts punching me in the head while I'm driving, a tactic he probably learned from his fucking dad. I pull over, Trey and Roadhouse drag his ass out of the car and throw him to the curb. I drop them off and head home. When I arrive home, I learn that Alan has been arrested and that he told the cops, and his parents, that I had abandoned him; which I did, but only because the motherfucker was beating on me. It was water under the bridge by the next day, at least for me.

Another time Alan and Roadhouse were getting stoned and playing video games at Alan's after school. Alan left his bag of weed open on the floor and his dad's dog Red ate the weed. Apparently Red got pretty baked. They said he ate a bunch of junk food they gave him and then just crashed. Roadhouse made sure to get the hell out of there before Alan's dad got home. There was nowhere for Alan to go.

Alan's dad gets home from work, "Red's acting a little strange. Alan, have you noticed Red acting a little funny today?"

"No, uh-uh." Alan is so fucking high.

"Maybe I should take him to the vet."

Alan's dad takes Red to the vet. An hour gos by. Alan's dad calls him from the vet, "Well it looks like Red's not gonna make it. If there's anything you can tell us about, maybe something that Red has ingested, or anything else that might be helpful, now would be the time."

"No, nothing. I can't think of anything dad." They both hang up.

Alan's dad shows back up at the house an hour or so later with the dog. "We found this in Red's stomach." Alan's dad holds up a gooey brown nug of Mexican dirt weed. Red is fine.

Alan made good in the end. He went to an alternative high school for fuck ups after his freshman year. Apparently, unlike normal high school, the teachers gave a shit there and Alan ended up graduating early. He would go on to get a degree in English. He now teaches honors English at a high school in the Houston area. Shit, all my friends I played music with made good after high school. I'm the only one who didn't get a degree, and I probably had the best shot out of all of them.

Chad had it the worst. His mom was addicted to crack cocaine and in and out of jail all the time. I guess him and his brothers were raised by their grandmother in their younger years, but she died and they were kind of on their own after that. Chad lived between friend's houses and his grandmother's old place during high school. He always had some shitty job. He was the oldest of three and tried to take care of his two younger brothers as best he could.

He worked at *Wendy's* for a while and had devised a scheme with a co-worker to steal money from the cash register, you know, to make up for the fact that they were getting paid $4.50 an hour. Every time a car ordered only things from the dollar menu at the drive through, Chad wouldn't ring up the sale. He instead would place a hash mark on a sheet of paper for every dollar-menu item sold and his buddy would make the food. At the end of their shift they would count up all the hashes, multiply that buy 1.07 and then take the sum out of the drawer. It was genius.

Chad moved into my old room at my folks' house when I moved to California. His mom had gotten clean, but expected him to pay rent to live in her dead mother's house while he was in college. Chad off-handedly mentions this to my mom while my dad was helping him with his car.

My mom, "Well you could just move in here rent free." Chad stayed for a couple years. It was nice to come home to visit and have my friend living in my old room. Somebody to hang with to break up the monotony of polite conversation with my folks.

Chad was a funny motherfucker. He could really get

under some people's skin. Shit, he might have been better at it than Bob. He certainly had more tact. I don't ever remember noticing people being pissed off at Chad, at least not for a long period of time. It did get kind of old being called a pussy fifty times a day everyday when you hung out with him, but I could deal with that.

Him and Alan made a hilarious pair on tour. We were at this party in Detroit back in 05' and Alan and Chad are both on the prowl. They're hitting on the same girl, so like a gentleman Alan poses a question to Chad, "Hey Chad, are you gonna fuck that girl in the pink sweater? Cuz if you're not gonna try to fuck her, then I'm gonna try to fuck her. But if you are trying to fuck her, then I'll back off." If I remember correctly Alan is in the hallway outside of the bathroom. The hallway leads into the kitchen. Chad is in the Kitchen. The girl in the pink sweater has just descended the stair case that lets out into the other side of the kitchen. Alan doesn't see her, but she hears him. Chad turns, puts his head down, and walks into the backyard saying nothing.

And then there was Trey, he fucking cracks me up. Trey actually voted for George W. Bush in 04'. That's right, he voted for George W. Bush after the invasions of Iraq and Afghanistan, and after it was totally apparent, beyond a shadow of a doubt, that the guy was a fucking moron. But Trey believes in Jesus and shit, so he votes Republican. I wonder if he voted for Trump.......

One time Trey was fucking with Chad on stage and Chad says into the mic, "This guy voted for George W. Bush." The crowd boos. Classic. I voted for Ralph Nader in 04'. I voted for Ralph Nader in 2000. Wasted my vote on Barack Obama in 08', and then voted for Ralph Nader again in 2012. I only threw away my vote once. Texas and California are never close.

Trey's parents had their issues too. His mom was a school teacher that liked her cheap bourbon. She was totally functional though, I never remember seeing her drunk or anything really. We of course drank the bourbon she kept under the kitchen sink on a regular basis.

His dad Tommy spent his days getting stoned and breeding geckos while watching Star Trek re-runs on VHS. He had lost his business doing foundations for beach houses in Galveston because he didn't pay his taxes. We'd go over there during school sometimes and smoke his dad's dope. His dad would inevitably show up at some point when we were hangin' round high as shit. "Trey, why aren't you in school?"

"Class was canceled."

"Bullshit class was canceled, and somebody's been in my room."

"Shut the fuck up, nobody's been in your room."

Tommy had this kind of make-shift security system set up with the door to his room. Something with empty toilet paper rolls and string. If anything was out of place when he got back from his errands, he would know Trey had come for his weed.

Trey's little brother Brian had down syndrome. I remember frequently picking Trey up to go party or do whatever we were doing with ourselves, and the scene at his house would always go a little something like this:

I'd be waiting at the front door, maybe chit chatting a little bit with his mom. "Hi Greg, how are you? What are you guys up to tonight?"

"Hi Mrs. Turner we're-"

Trey, "Shut up don't talk to her."

"Oh Trey come on now," his mom would say.

Trey, "Shut up."

Tommy, "Goddammit Trey, don't talk to your mother that way!"

"Shut up, shut the fuck up. I'll be right back Greg." Trey walks down the hall to the bathroom. "Goddammit Brian I told you to close the door when you're jackin' off."

Trey dated Karen's sister Megan, I guess that's how I met Karen. Trey referred to Karen as Marolyn Manson, I guess because she was so skinny. She wasn't goth or anything. We were some mean bastards. I remember making out with Karen in Trey's bedroom. We were in love immediately.

Me and Karen almost got married back in 2000. It was Superbowl Sunday and I threw a party at my apartment in Dickinson. That's the next town south from League City on Interstate 45. None of us gave a shit about football or anything, but it was a good excuse to get drunk. Tim and Richard from my then job at *Pearle Vision* came over, and Sam, Roadhouse, Vik, and Chad were also in attendance.

Somewhere around midnight Tim and Richard take off. After they leave, me and Karen decide we want to get married right then, that night. So we drive around Houston trying to find an all night wedding chapel. We have zero luck, so we do the most obvious and perfectly logical thing that there is to do. We all piled into Sam's van and headed for Vegas. I pass out in the back and wake up in Fort Stockton around 9am. Just slightly hungover. I call my work, "Hey Tim, I'm not gonna be able to make it in today."

"Oh man Shag, you gotta come in today, we're already getting slammed."

"Man, don't get me wrong, I'd love to, but even if I turned the van I'm in around right now, I wouldn't get there until the store was closing. I'm not gonna be able to make it in for the rest of the week actually." I go on to explain the brilliant decision me and my compatriots have made the previous evening in our collective drunken stupors. Everybody else with a job calls in.

We drive west for the better part of the day through New Mexico then Arizona. In eastern Arizona we pull off the interstate onto a government road just for the hell of it. We leave the van and climb a mesa. Once at the top, we smoke a joint and realize what a colossally bad idea this all was. Funny how marijuana will do that; make you realize that you're an idiot and all the decisions you made when you were drunk were not necessarily good ones.

The sun is setting and we realize we are going to be lost in the desert at night without a flashlight. Sam races to the van and gets the headlights on just before the sun sets. The rest of us find our way back to the van, then head east back to Texas. We pull into a truck stop somewhere in West Texas and sleep in the parking lot that night. It was cold. We get up the next day and I drive. Chad and Vik are throwing fire crackers out the back window of the van and drinking Natural Light. Sam is pissed off because Vikram has pissed in the drink shaker he got for his birthday. Sam throws it out the window.

We pull into San Antonio mid-day and there is a

torrential downpour going on, so we decide to visit The Alamo. We sneak wine coolers in and get drunk. That evening we get back to Dickinson unmarried but still very much in love.

-THE HISTORY OF VIKRAM-

Vikram is four years older than me. He's the son of Indian immigrants. His mother worked for UTMB (University of Texas Medical Branch) in Galveston and I don't know what his father did. He started college at University of Texas in Austin the same year me and Roadhouse started high school at Clear Creek High in League City. His freshman year of college, in every way, was a classic case. Strict parents from a foreign land. Never got to do anything during high school except hit the books. Then, freedom! He moves three hours west of his parents and their rules. Vikram parties non-stop. Needless to say he flunked all of his classes, but unlike other kids in his situation Vikram did not limp home with his tail between his legs. Vik wasn't going down without a fight. He had bigger plans for his academic future. Vikram knew some kid who worked in the dean's office who could help him fake his "report cards" home (or whatever they call it in college- I don't know. I only went a little; a very long time ago). The kid in the office would intercept any mail headed to the Bot residence and replace it with a glowing review of Vikram's achievements in higher education. His plan was, "I fucked up my first semester, but I'm gonna pull it out in the spring." Of course he doesn't. He continues to skip class and party all while sending home fabricated reports, until one day, the truth slips through with a letter unnoticed by his man on the inside.

His father calls on the phone. "Vikram, what the hell is going on here? You're failing all your classes Vikram!"

"No dad it must be some mistake.....Uh I don't know."

So Vik goes and has his friend help him fabricate a new kind of mail for his parents. A letter personally from the dean of UT, seal and all, on the dean's stationary. The letter says something to the effect of, "We hope you will accept our apologies for the error, Mr. and Mrs. Bot. Here are Vikram's actual grades." Now that shit worked, but Vik did not. By the end of the school year Vikram had gone from academic probation to flunking out miserably. He had to go home and tell his parents the truth. I don't know how that went, but I imagine that could be a story in itself. But I never heard it.

So Vik is back in League City. He starts delivering pizzas for a living in his old Toyota van that has a piece of cardboard for one of the back windows. That van ran forever, he never fixed the window. Roadhouse rides along with him sometimes on his deliveries and gets drunk with him while he works, they were quite the pair.

It was a fortuitous moment the day I went into *DJ's Liquor* in League City with Vikram. We chatted with Sonny, the Indian guy who ran the place, and before I knew it, I had a place to buy liquor, beer, and cigarettes from the age of 17 on. A fucking goldmine for a teenager!

One night, my junior year of high school, I sneak out of my parents house. I go and pick up Vik and Roadhouse and we decide to go around to all the grocery stores in the area and steal beer. It was a Tuesday night if I remember correctly. I had school the next day. The other two did not. So we hit all the 24 hour grocery stores, especially *Albertsons*, which has a walk-in cooler. You walk in, slam a beer, put as many beers in your pants and coat as you can fit, maybe open a bag of chips and a little dip, have a little snack on your way out. What kind of idiot came up with the walk-in cooler? Oh, just give a bunch of punk ass kids a nice discrete place to steal shit or just get drunk right there. You don't see any walk in coolers in Oakland.

Anyways, we do this for a couple hours. Driving around, drinking beer, stealing beer, until surprise! We get pulled over. We stuck out like a sore thumb in my sky blue, 62' *Plymouth Valiant*. Cool car until you realize that every cop in town knows your car, your friends, and what kind of shit you get into with those friends in that car. They could spot me comin' from a mile away.

They pull us over in the parking lot of an *Academy* (a sporting goods store). All of a sudden there are four cop cars on the scene and eight cops. They separate the three of us. Me in the back of one car, Vik in another, and Roadhouse is posted up behind the car that Vikram is in. So I'm sitting in the back of this cop car, half drunk and pissed off thinking, "Damn this is gonna be some shit." When all of a sudden, I hear a sound like a woman screaming. I look up and House is on the ground howling and holding his crotch. My parents show up right then and pull me out of the cop car. Jeremy's mom gets there. He's screaming at this fucking pig. "I WANT YOUR BADGE NUMBER YOU FUCKING PIG!"

Jeremy's mom Nancy pleads, "Shut up Jeremy! Let's go home." Cop puts his hand over his badge and another cop steps in front of him to protect the brotherhood.

Apparently this fucking pig was searching Roadhouse and he got a little friendly. Put his hand on Jeremy's package and asks, "What's this?" Roadhouse mouthed off to him and the cop crushed his testicles. That fucker was limping around for a week, the poor bastard.

So me and Roadhouse are headed home and Vikram is headed to jail. They wrote me and Jeremy minor in possession of alcohol tickets and I don't know what they charged Vik with, but it wasn't contributing to the delinquency of a minor. I ride home with my mom in her minivan and my dad drives my car. We get to the house and my mom is pretty calm but my dad is fucking pissed. I'm at the top of the stairs and my dad is at the bottom. We start to argue. I tell him to fuck off or something to that effect. He rushes me and before I know it we are on the floor and my dad is punching me in the back. Not very hard, mind you. Neither of us were fighters. I was shocked. I say, "What are you doing?"

"I don't know." My dad goes to bed. I go to bed. That was the only time my dad ever hit me, and I probably deserved it.

The Summer after my junior year of high school Vikram's parents took a trip to India with his sister. They were gone for two weeks, so of course all our friends pretty much lived at Vik's folks beach house while they were away. Except for me, I had an 11pm curfew until I turned 18. The house was on Tiki Island, a small community near the mainland side of Galveston Bay right off Interstate 45. Kegs were rolled in and people started getting fucked up. Especially Vikram, of course. At first he was a little uptight about the whole thing. Don't go into this room or that room, cigarette butts in this bucket, trash here, bottles and cans there, etc...... By day three Vik was throwing his parents good china into Galveston Bay while yelling, "Fuck it all!" at the top of his lungs. People were smoking dope and fucking all over that house.

His parents had two pet cocker spaniels, Lady and The Tramp. Vik loved Disney cartoons. I don't know if he named them or not, but I do know this. Lady fucking loved alcohol. She hung out by the keg 24/7 just wandering around in circles licking up spilled beer. By the time his parents got back from India that beach house was thoroughly destroyed. We cleaned it up as best we could, but there was really no un-fucking up that place. We passed Vik's parents on the road as they were returning from their trip. We got out just in the nick of time.

The next day Vik gets a call from his dad. His parents have been assessing the damage. "Vikram! What the hell has been going on here Vikram? All of our china is missing, there are semen stains all over your sister's bed, and there is something wrong with the dog." Vik's mother had taken his 12 year old sister's sheets to the lab at UTMB to be analyzed. Lady ended up dying a couple days later and his parents never saw their china again.

I think it might have been after this episode that Vik's parents sent him to India for college. He went unwillingly and they made sure he didn't have the means to escape. He told me stories about monkeys breaking into his apartment and gangsters extorting money from his drunk ass. He wound up owing money, somehow, to organized crime in India. They had him empty his bank account then beat the shit out of him and left him in a parking garage. After a couple months of this Vik was begging Bob to figure out a way to get him back to the states and out of this whole mess. So Bob got everybody to chip in and we all bought Vikram a plane ticket back to Houston. I don't think I threw in actually. Can't remember...........

Vik gets home and calls his parents from Bob's house, "Hey dad I'm back in League City, over at Bob's house."

"Oh that's a good one Vikram, very good. You wont get me this time, I'll call you right back."

Rob used to prank call Vik's dad on a regular basis. It was cruel but also pretty funny. He would put that shit on speaker phone and we'd all sit and listen while Rob strung along Vik's dad with one complex charade after another. He got him enough times that Vik's dad had learned not to trust any phone calls that seemed in the least bit suspicious. So Vik's dad calls Bob's house. Vik answers the phone. The shit hits the fan at the Bot residence once again.

In November of my senior year I turn 18 and tell my parents to fuck off. They do, God bless them. Vikram has gotten himself a job at the *Citgo* gas station next to the Meadow Bend subdivision in League City. He is living with Bob and Bob's parents. He can jump the back fence, walk across the highway, and he's at work. He works the graveyard shift exclusively. Indians run the gas station and they make the mistake of thinking that Vikram is one of them. He is not. He is "Dick-Scum" now. That was the nickname that Bob had bestowed upon him.

Now this was another goldmine for our little crew of fuck-up teenagers. We had been given the keys to the castle. The castle of: Free booze, free cigarettes, free gas, free porn, free shitty gas station food, and free lottery tickets which were always cashed in whenever a winner came up. At least that's how Bob saw it with the lottery tickets. Vik had that job for one glorious spring month in

1999. Everyone hung out there. Roadhouse's brother Josh made a short film with their mom's video camera. It was about a robbery at the Citgo. I never saw it.

Vik would drink beer at the register while he was working. He'd piss in the sink back there when he thought he couldn't leave his post. We would look at porn and get fucked up in the cooler. One night Trevor asks Chad, "Let me ask you something Chad, how many times a week do you masturbate?"

"I don't know......a regular amount of times I guess."

I pass out drunk in the cooler one night and they take pictures of me with a stolen disposable camera. I'm in a compromising position with an open bottle of pickled pigs feet. Cops come in the store sometimes. "Nothing happening here officer. It's totally normal for a bunch of teenagers to be in this gas station in the middle of the night on a weekday."

Roadhouse quits his job at the waterfront running rides. "Why would I work? The Citgo has everything I need." I had to give it to him, he did have a point.

This drug dealer named Armando starts trading Vikram cocaine for beer. Armando pulls up one night in a limo with strippers. House and Vik take a joy ride with him. Vik just says fuck it and closes the store for an hour. At the end of that beautiful, beautiful month, Vikram's employers do inventory and promptly fire his ass and garnish his wages. I guess Phil went up there with him and tried to get more of his paycheck, but I don't know if anything ever came of it. Shit, I would have taken the whole fucking thing if I ran that *Citgo*, we robbed that place blind.

I coast real hard my last semester of high school. I

really only bother going to English 4, that's the only credit I need to graduate. The rest I say, fuck it. I have $1,500 saved from working at *Walgreens* the last two years. Well, two different *Walgreens*. I got fired from the one in League City for not bothering to show up to work. A month or two after that I run out of money, so I head down to the *Walgreens* in Dickinson and get a job there. The assistant manager of the League City store, a Hawaiian named Patrick O'Brian, has been given the Dickinson store. We had always been tight. He was a real sleaze ball. His wife got arrested for writing herself prescriptions that she tried to fill at the store he worked at. He married a fucking genius. I start working 32 hours a week instead of 12 after the beer stealing incident with the crushed balls. By Christmas of 98' I had a nice chunk of money saved up and I quit that job. The last five months of my senior year were great. I blew threw that money and ran out right about the time I graduated. Which might not have happened had it not been for my mother's expert skills in manipulation. Especially over the phone.

I get called into the principal's office one afternoon toward the end of my senior year. Principal asks me, "How have you been getting away with this?"

"Getting away with what?" I ask.

"You haven't been attending school. There's a class here you've only been to once!"

"I just didn't go to a lot of those classes cuz I didn't need them to graduate."

"Well this is unacceptable. You're going to have to do two weeks of in school suspension to graduate."

"The hell I am," I think. I don't give a fuck if I

graduate high school or not. Then he makes the mistake of calling my mother, Barbie. This is gonna be great........

"Mrs. Ashley, your son's attendance this semester has been poor to say the least. He has only really been attending one of his classes." Bla bla bla. Some shit about my GPA and other nonsense that never ended up mattering anyways. Then Barbie takes over. The call lasts for about an hour. After his little spiel the only words this poor guy can get in are, "uh huh, yes, oh that's interesting, OK, huh." At the end of all this my principal conjures up a rousing speech the likes of which this world would never hear before or after this day. "Alright Mrs. Ashley, we are gonna knock Gregory's ISS down to two days and we'll drop all the classes he is failing to bring his GPA back up. Mrs. Ashley, I want you to imagine your son is in Vietnam. He's just finished his tour of duty. He is waiting for the chopper, "graduation", that is going to extract him from the jungle. The Vietcong are closing in on him. He might get his leg blown off, maybe he loses an arm. But Mrs. Ashley, we are going to get your son on that chopper. WE WILL GET HIM ON THAT CHOPPER!"

So I graduate. I'm jobless and broke. My mom starts going around to all the different places she shops at and brings me home a stack of applications. I look at none of them. Then one day she is getting her glasses adjusted at *Pearle Vision* up in Webster. She talks up the manager, "You should hire my son. He's real smart and a hard worker." Which is possibly true at this point in my life. So they hire me. I start working in the lab making lenses for eyeglasses. I meet Karen that summer. By the fall I had saved enough money to get my own apartment. I move out, move into the Pine Forest apartment complex in Dickinson. Karen is a year younger than me so she is still in high school. In January she turns 18, gets a settlement from a car wreck she was in when she was 15, and moves in with me. I can't remember if she graduated or not.

Vikram moves in. He lives on the couch in the living room. I soon realize I have to charge him by the week instead of the month or he'll never be able to come up with the rent. He has a new job every week. He has probably held more shit jobs than anyone else in the history of mankind. He works at: *Jack In The Box, Krogers, Pappasitos, The Olive Garden*, every shitty pizza place in town, fucking *Citgo*, and the list goes on. He weaves elaborate webs of lies for his employers when he wakes up with a hangover and just wants to get drunk again. He tells me, "It's better to say your uncle died than your father. If you say your dad died, then you have to keep the sad act going forever. It's exhausting."

Karen never bothers to chip in on the rent. She hangs out eating frozen dinners and watching stolen cable in the bedroom while Vik sits on the couch and drinks. I come home to a dirty apartment on a regular basis. I have to do the dishes in the bathtub because they are piled up so high in, and around, the kitchen sink that you just don't have the room to wash all that shit in there.

Vik invents "The Pickletini" which consists of pickle juice and vodka with a pickle garnish. All we had in the fridge was white bread, roaches, and pickles. Vik was creative and Karen loved her pickles.

This guy moves in upstairs. We call him Ganglee. He sells drugs. We take drugs. We get drunk on booze from

DJ's Liquor. These five Mexican dudes who work construction move in next door. Five guys in a one bedroom apartment. One of them sells cocaine. We buy cocaine. One day two of them come over and we all get fucked up together. The next night they come back and the coke dealer one says to Karen, "I'm sorry, my brother stole your panties. Here they are, I'm sorry."

Karen, "What the fuck?!"

Then the brother offers her cocaine for a pair of her panties. Karen agrees, hands him a pair of underwear from her dresser drawer, but the brother isn't satisfied, "No, I want those, the dirty ones."

"Fuck you," is Karen's reply this time. We stop hanging with the Mexicans, but sometimes we eat the tacos they are constantly grilling on the front lawn. Really not bad guys actually, and good tacos. Panties guy just probably hadn't gotten laid in a while or something.

We had an incurable roach problem. We have to bang out our shoes every morning, to expel all the baby roaches. We have keg parties in that apartment with jungle juice, a mixture of *Everclear* and fruit juice. Trey calls it "Bitch Water". No one ever complains. The apartment complex has an obvious form of segregation going on. White people with kids in the front. Mexicans and dirt bags like us in the middle. Blacks on the other side of the stream in the back.

I start going to community college a year after high school so my parents start paying the rent. I drop from full to part-time work at *Pearle Vision*. My boss Tim becomes a good friend, as well as this other guy that works there named Richard. Richard calls me Shag because of my hair.

One year, on Tim's birthday, the three of us get trashed at Tim's and decide we should get some coke. Tim keeps saying, "You guys gotta go to work tomorrow, cuz I'm not goin' in."

Me and Richard hit the road. We pick up some crazy white trash bitch. I don't know where. She directs us to this trailer at the end of Deats Road in Dickinson. We go in and Richard starts acting like he knows the drug dealers for some reason. "Chicken George. You don't remember Chicken George man? Ha gum man."

Anyways, we come out with some shit and hop back into my truck. Hit the road back to Tim's. We get back and it turns out Richard has bought crack. Now at this point, due to the machine of propaganda in the USA, I'm a little afraid of smoking crack. "Cant we just crush it up and snort it?" I ask.

Richard, "Na Shag you gotta smoke it."

Me, "OK."

Tim, "I'll get the bong."

We put a little Brillo in the bowl and we're off to the races. I don't last more than an hour at work the next day. Richard toughed out the whole eight.

Some months later me and Chad are getting drunk at my apartment and I remember the crack trailer. We head down Deats road. Knock on the door. "Hey man, can we get some shit?"

Crack dealer, "Shiii, how many rocks you want white boy?"

"Two?"

"Ah-ight." Dude pulls a couple rocks out of his mouth and hands them to me.

"Cool, thanks."

"Put them in your lip."

"Na, I'll just put them in my pocket."

"Put them in your fucking mouth!"

"OK." Cracks in my mouth now. We drive back to my apartment and smoke crack. End of story.

Eventually I kick Karen and Vik out of my apartment. Me and Karen break up and Vikram starts living at Chad's for a while. Chad's mom was in jail for smoking crack at the time.

Vik moved to Tacoma in 2000 with Josh, Bob and Trevor. They had a band called *Vegetable F.* Vik had been on and off junk since he moved to Tacoma. He had swapped the booze for the H. He was probably doing both, in fact I know he was.

He moved to Boston in the mid/late 00's and started a punk band with his girlfriend called *The Mess Me Ups.* Man his old lady was nuts. She had trained him, at home, to do the same job she had. It had something to do with accounting for a moving business. There was an opening at her work, so she taught him the software and made him a fake resume. When he went in for the interview he aced it of course. Vik is actually a really smart guy, and he knew exactly how to answer everything they were going to throw at him. He got the job. Smart woman to get Vik a descent job he wouldn't just be able to walk away from at the drop of a hat. She wasn't gonna pay for all the dope herself. She had to put Vik to work.

Me and Scott and Brandon (from Athens, OH) stayed with them in Boston on tour once. It was total chaos. Vik gave me his cat's bed for a pillow. I woke up the next morning and my right eye was swelled up so big it looked like I was that fucker Sloth from *Goonies*. After the swelling subsided I had a sty in that eye for over a year.

East coast or West coast Vik always found junk. He couldn't escape. Vikram came to visit Oakland in either 2010 or 2011. Him and his lady had parted ways and he was living outside of Boston now going back to school to be a radiology technician or something. He was on his spring break I think. He came out for a week or so. It was fun, we partied, did a bunch of coke and got drunk. As the week wore on I had bands to record, and he started staying in the motels down the block from me above the liquor store on San Pablo. Then he started shooting dope. He knew what kind of neighborhood I lived in. He planned that shit. This was his heroin vacation. He got right into the flow of San Pablo ave. Same as Tacoma or Boston, junkies know where to get their fix.

For the rest of the week, I didn't see Vik, until I drove him to the airport to go back to Massachusetts. I went up to his room above the liquor store. I was surprised, it wasn't too much different than a *Motel 6*. Kind of crappy, but nicer than where I lived in the warehouse, and there were plenty of junkies there too. He offered me his old cotton balls you draw the dope through after you cook the tar in a spoon. You put the needle against the cotton ball to filter what you're about to shoot into your vein. I only ever snorted it, and let me tell you, dripping black tar heroin down your nasal passages is some nasty shit. Puting something into my vein is where I draw the line, especially some toxic cooked up tar. Anyways, there was heroin left in the cotton balls, but I passed. Dropped him off at the airport.

I get a call from Vik the next day, "Greg, I'm starting to get sick. The guy I was buying dope off of out there said if I Western Union him some money he'll mail me some heroin."

"That sounds like a bad idea Vik, don't send that guy any money. He's gonna rip you off. Just tough it out and start over." Easy for me to say.

Next day, "I sent him the money."

"How much money did you send him Vik?"

"200 bucks."

"I don't think you're gettin' that dope Vikram."

Two days go by, "He hasn't sent me the shit. I'm going fucking crazy! I'm getting a plane ticket and coming back out there to kill that motherfucker!"

"Vik you're not coming back out here. You're already through the worst of it. Just let it go." I don't think I've spoken to Vik since then. Roadhouse offered me his number the other day. Tom in Houston gave it to him so he'd know when not to answer the phone. Maybe I should have taken it. I'd talk to Vik if he called. It's been 7 years or so........

-ROB, SHROOMS & LSD-

We all loved psilocybin mushrooms. Out in southeast and central Texas, psilocybin mushrooms grow naturally on cow shit. You have to be a bit cautious, mind you, to pick the right ones, not every mushroom that grows on a cow patty will make you trip. You could end up picking a death cap if you weren't careful. The safest ones to pick were the ones we referred to as "dick heads". They are dark gray and look as the name suggests.

My parents had cattle and sometimes we would pick the ones that grew out at their ranch up in Kosse. Down in League City, us kids knew about a couple good fields that always produced a decent yield. It was always important, as Rob would say to, "tap the cap" after you picked the shroom. I don't know if this really did anything, but the thinking was that if you tapped the cap, spores would be released down onto the cow shit to promote the growth of future psilocybin mushrooms.

We'd go out in the middle of the night, wandering around on some strangers property with flashlights and trash bags hunting for the nights entertainment. I'm sure it was a strange and somewhat unsettling sight to wake up in the middle of the night, as a rancher, and see a bunch of kids with flashlights pointed to the ground methodically wandering your field. Maybe they'd know what we were up to, maybe not. It never happened to me personally, but there was many a story of kids looking for shrooms and being chased off a rancher's property at gun point.

These wild shrooms aren't nearly as strong as the lab grown variety. I learned this fun fact the hard way about a year or two after moving to California. There were three of us signed up for this trip. Me, Eric and Michelle. I bought three 8ths of lab grown shrooms, and we each took a whole 8th. I looked at the baggies when I was buying the drugs and thought, "This ain't shit." Some tough guy I was. The three of us tripped in an attic apartment that resembled a doll house. None of us knew each other very well back then. Eric is a close friend now and I see Michelle every once in a while.

So, new friends, strange environment and a heroic dose of psychedelics. Michelle had the time of her life. She just sat there and laughed at me and Eric while we cried and drug ourselves back and forth across the carpet. I took five showers. Didn't help me come down at all. Then I completely lost my identity for an hour or two. I just sat on a bed looking out a window wondering who I was, and where I was, and why I was there. It was actually kind of peaceful in a way to completely lose your sense of self. "I just was," as they say. Fucking confusing.

Anyways the wild shrooms in Texas aren't that strong, but if you take enough of them you'll trip all the same, and that's what Rob loved to do. It was a free ride. Rob even brought home one of his favorite turds in a shoe box which he hid underneath his bed. His dad found it and was perplexed. "Why does my son have a piece of cow shit in a shoe box under his bed?" I think it produced. I don't remember what he told his parents.

Rob, when I first met him, had just returned home from UT. He was in the same class as Vikram. Unlike Vik he finished school, well minus one credit supposedly. I don't know if he ever finished his degree or not, but close enough. He was working delivering pizzas, a job he had for a number of years before he started installing cable. We hung out a lot, drank beer, took drugs, typical shit.

One day before his shift Rob decides to do something special with his latest batch of mushrooms. He makes a pasta. Spaghetti and meatballs with psilocybin mushrooms. He whips up his dinner, eats a portion, puts the leftovers in the fridge, and is off to work. I don't have any idea why you would wanna deliver pizzas tripping, but Rob was crazy like that.

Around midnight or so his shift ends and he heads home, still kinda tripping from dinner. Rob gets back to his folks place, the lights are out, it's quiet, he enters the house. As he walks through the kitchen his mother emerges from the shadows. "Rob, make sure not to eat any of that pasta in the fridge. Your father and I feel very strange."

Rob walks into the living room. His father is glued to the lazy boy. "You doin' alright dad?"

"It's not all that unpleasant," his dad replies.

Not all that unpleasant. Man, one time i took five hits of acid on Halloween at my apartment in Dickinson. Wasn't the least bit unpleasant. Chad was there, Nick was there, fucking Beastmaster was there. Beastmaster took shrooms, everybody else took a lot of acid. I think Roadhouse and Trey were there, but I'm not totally certain. We were sitting around listening to psychedelic music just having a good time, and then these guys that went to college with Lauren came over. It's Halloween mind you, and I'm trippin' balls. One of these jokers is dressed like the guy from *A Clockwork Orange*, Another looks like a hippy, and the last dude just looks like a fuckin' square. They're milling around the living room where we are hanging out, fucking bothering us. If it isn't bad enough I gotta trip with Beastmaster, I gotta deal with these fuckers too. They are asking Beastmaster if he, "has anymore of that strange fungi?"

"No," says Beastmaster.

They hang for a while and then it's time for them to leave. Lauren and Karen are gonna go to some party with them, I don't remember where. So they get ready to leave and we are saying our goodbyes and I go a little overboard on the conversation. Fucking dumb-ass that I am, but it's not that bad, what happened was an honest mistake.........could have happened to anybody. I say, "Hey I get your costume, you're the guy from *A Clockwork Orange*. And you're a fuckin' hippie, but what are you dressed up as? What's your costume?"

Art Students, "Um......We're not wearing costumes."

Apparently Karen realized what was happening from the first words out of my mouth and she tried to shut me up. Didn't work. They go to the party.

-THE BOYLANDS & SO ON-

The Boylands were a clan of indigenous white trash to the League City area. The last of the best. I don't know how long they had been there but four of my friends were Boylands. You had: Phil, son of Jack. Rachel and Shana, daughters of Jimmy, and Graham, who's mother was Jack and Jimmy's cousin. Of course Jack and Jimmy were notorious drunks and/or wife beaters. Jimmy may not have hit Carla (Rachel and Shana's mom) but Jack certainly hit his wife. The story goes that one day Jack was beating on Phil's mom and Phil knocked him out with some kind of homemade nightstick. Phil loved his mom. Shit, he lived with her well into his twenties. His girlfriend even moved in with them. Phil, "Why would I get a job and move out? My mom cooks. There's no rules. It's free rent."

I barely ever saw her. I just knew that we could do whatever the fuck we wanted over at Phil's house. We could smoke pot and cigarettes in Phil's room. His mom didn't care. We could drink beer in the house. His mom didn't care. Phil had a weed plant in the backyard. His mom didn't care. The neighbors cared though, and when the plant got taller than the fence, the police came and confiscated it and wrote Phil a ticket.

We smoked lots of dope at Phil's house. Early in high school I bought my weed from this guy named Wes. He was older than me and had an apartment. Real scumbag, a fuckin' asshole. Everybody hated Wes. Every time you bought weed from him you had to stay at his apartment for at least thirty minutes. He didn't want too many people coming in and out of his place in a short amount of time.

Wes was paranoid. It was Texas.

He had this retarded fucking system of code language that you had to use when calling to buy drugs. If you wanted a dime you would say, "Is it OK if I stop by in ten minutes?" Half ounce, "Half hour?" Ounce, "Come over in an hour?" But it always backfired because dip-shits would call and say, "Is it OK if I come over in an hour? OK, I'll be there in twenty minutes."

Wes always made you smoke with him. You had to match bowls with him. I was over there once and Wes secretly sprayed mace in the corner of his apartment because he thought it would be funny to see everyone cry while they were stoned.

Another time Wes was over at Rob's and as always, we were all getting high together. There was maybe six or seven of us. Wes goes to use the can, and when he gets up, twenty bucks falls out of his pocket. I grab it. Wes comes out, says his goodbyes, and takes off. I show everyone the twenty bucks. Everyone is stoked. Fuck Wes! Wes comes back realizing he is missing twenty bucks. We all play dumb, he leaves. I go to the gas station and buy a carton of cigarettes. I give everybody who smokes a pack or two. That's back in the good old days when a carton of cigarettes was only twenty bucks. I felt like *Robin Hood* or something. Stealing from the man and giving back to my brothers and sisters. Big mistake.

I guess a few nights later Wes cornered Tanya at a party and got it out of her that I was the one that had stolen his money. No mention of the cigarettes she smoked bought on his stolen dime. Anyways, I understood, Wes was an imposing figure. She probably thought he was gonna rape her or something.

So Wes starts showing up at my work. Coming into *Walgreens* asking me where the razor blades are and stupid shit like that, trying to intimidate me or something. He starts calling my mom and threatening her because I stole his money. My mom suggests, "Maybe Gregory can wash your car a couple of times or something." After a while I give Wes the twenty dollars back. I might have ended up having to give him twice that for all I remember, but it got rid of him anyways. Eventually I find other people to buy weed from, thank God.

Anyways, back to Phil. Phil knew how to fight. I boxed him once for about twenty seconds. He played with me and let me try to punch him for the first fifteen, then he decked me in the side of the head. He could have hit me harder, but he held back cuz he's a nice guy. That was it for me though. I threw in the towel after one punch from him, dazed and unsteady on my feet.

He fucked up Bob at least a couple times. Bob's mouth got his ass beat more than once. One time Bob punched me in the face at a party for hitting on Paola, I was pleasantly surprised to hear that later that evening an overweight frat boy fell on him during an altercation and broke his collar bone. After that, Bob was nice to everybody for a couple months, then his collar bone healed, and he went back to doing what he did best. Being a fucking asshole. But we all loved him, how could we not? He was hilarious, when he wasn't picking on you.

Phil beat Bob's ass in Trevor's front yard one night. Trevor's grandmother had a garden in the front of their place with these big square concrete stepping stones leading up to the front door. Phil beat Bob's face into one of the stones and Bob ended up with a right angle imprinted on his forehead for a week or so.

I think to fight, the most important skill to have, is knowing what it feels like to get the living shit beaten out of you and not have it be a big deal. People that have this usually have an abusive parent or an older brother. At least in my experience it's one of the two or both. I didn't have this. I haven't really ever been in a fight. This kid Kervin hit me in the back of the head on the last day of school in 7th grade and Bob punched me in the face at that party. Other than that, my parents didn't beat me and my older sister didn't. So I can't fight. Phil knew how to fight probably because his dad beat the shit out of him on a regular basis. With all the times Bob got his ass beat you'd have thought he would have learned to fight too, but he didn't.

Bullies create other bullies for better or worse, and Texas is full of them. It's a state founded and run by bullies, and those ignorant bastards are proud of that shit. Texas gave it to Bob and Bob was kind enough to pass it on to the rest of us. When I first moved to California I was flabbergasted. Why is everybody here such a fucking pussy? What gives? It took me about a decade to realize that people were just nice and I was a fucking dick. Don't get me wrong, there are plenty of assholes in California too, just a different kind of asshole, and most of the assholes out on the west coast are transplants like me anyways.

-TREVOR & THE STAR WARS ACTION FIGURE-

In the late 90's all three *Star Wars* films were re-released in theaters. In January of 97', *A New Hope*. February, *The Empire Strikes Back* and in March, *Return Of The Jedi*. When *A New Hope* comes out me and House and Josh and Trevor skip school and go to the first showing on the first day. I take acid. When the text starts to inch it's way up the screen and the music begins, the acid kicks in. It was endlessly entertaining, I had the giggles the whole film. Not many visuals but still a great time. I only took one hit, and thank God for that considering the subsequent events of that day.

When we left the theater and I walked out into the world, everything was bright and surreal. I couldn't drive my car so Josh did. We went to Trevor's and started hitting the bong on the side of the garage like we always did. Around four o'clock Trevor's grandma comes out of the house with the cordless phone and says, "Greg, your mother's on the phone." Shit, I think. What does she know? I'm still tripping, I dropped the acid around noon or something. I'm only halfway through my trip.

I take the cordless and....... yep, it's my mom, "I know you skipped school today. Come home right now." Couldn't argue with that. I don't remember how she found out but she did. So I drive home. What else was I supposed to do? It wasn't the last time I would drive while tripping, but it was the first.

I get home and we start arguing, then all of a sudden she says something to the effect of, "What are you talking about?"

I say, "I don't know. I'm going up to my room."

"We'll talk about this more when your father gets home."

So I wait........I sit and wait. Tripping my balls off........I wait. I hear the garage door open, Dad is home. I hear the back door open, then I hear, "What the hell? Gregory!" I guess now I gotta argue with this motherfucker. Now I don't remember how that went, but probably similar to the argument with my mom. Then it's dinner time. My family always ate dinner together around 6pm. Most of the time with Joe Morgan in attendance.

Joe was an old Texas rancher that had worked at Lockheed Martin with my dad. I guess they got along pretty well cuz they remained friends even after my dad left that job to work at NASA. My father was a cost analyst. I have no idea what old Joe Morgan's position was at Lockheed, but I do know he fought in the second world war. Joe joined The Air Force at 17 and flew bombing missions over Western Europe. He was a tail gunner. If you've ever seen the movie *Memphis Belle*, that was the kind of plane Joe was in. At some point his plane was shot down over occupied France. He escaped back to England with the help of The French Underground. All this when he was just a teenager. I suppose that's the only time in life when a government can convince a seemingly normal person to do something so monumentally fucking stupid and suicidal.

Joe, per my mother's request, taught me how to slaughter and gut a rabbit when I was ten or so. "First you have to kill it." Joe pulls a hammer out and beats the poor thing over the head until it stops breathing. "Then you skin it." We walk to a tree in the backyard that has a piece of wire hanging off one of the branches. He ties the wire around one of the rabbit's legs. He pulls out his pocket knife and cuts around both the rabbit's legs and across it's groin. The fur peels off like nothing. It's like the rabbit was wearing a tight sweater or something. Then he cuts off the head and guts it. The rabbit is twitching the whole time he is doing this, by the way, but he assures me it is very dead. "That's just nerves," he says. I wonder if I have it in me to beat an animal to death with a hammer and then skin and gut it with a pocket knife. I certainly ate it so I suppose I should have the balls to kill it.

So I'm sitting there tripping with mom, dad, sister, and Joe eating dinner. The corn was the hardest thing to get down. I could feel every kernel slide unwillingly down my throat and into my stomach which didn't want anything to do with food at this point. It's no fun eating while you're tripping, especially when you're doing it with your parents, who are pissed off at you, and you have to act like nothing is up on top of everything else. After dinner I vaguely remember leaving the house in some frantic dash. Trying to run away I guess. I only got as far as the edge of the yard before my dad ran after me and changed my mind. The drugs finally wore off and I went to bed. I think the whole skipping school thing that day blew over pretty quick. I got caught doing that so frequently that it must have.

In February, *Empire* comes out. I don't have a story for this one. Lost in the ether I suppose. Don't know if we went day or night, but I'm sure we went on the first day.

March and it's *Return of the Jedi*. This time we

definitely don't bother with the matinée. We go to the evening showing of *Return of the Jedi* on the first day. Josh and Shanelle head to the theater in Josh's car first. Me, Trevor and Jeremy hang back in my *Plymouth Valiant* and hit the bong. I have named the bong *The Enterprise*. I'm a Trekkie OK. We have each chosen our characters. I, of course, am *Captain Kirk*. It's my bong and my car. Trevor is *Warf*, and I believe Roadhouse is *Spock*.

We get high and end up at the theater after Josh and Shanelle. We find seats behind them. Now Trevor is one of the biggest *Star Wars* fans around. He's read the books. He's seen the movies a hundred times. He has the action figures. Shanelle turns to look back at us. "Trevor." Slowly, mockingly. "Look what I got Trevor." Boom! It's a special edition *Luke Skywalker* in storm trooper garb action figure. They gave them out to the first fifty people who showed up for the film.

A guy a few seats away says, "Hey, I'll give you fifty bucks for that right now." Shanelle hands him the toy. Trevor is steaming.

A month or two later a few of us are hanging out in Josh's room smoking pot. I think Phil was there. Phil was definitely there if we were smoking pot. Phil loved him some of somebody else's weed. "Fire it up Greg, we're all friends here," Phil would say. Josh pulls out the Skywalker figure to show off to Phil. Also a *Star Wars* fanatic. Phil looks it over, "That's just a regular *Luke Skywalker* figure."

Josh takes the doll, "No it's special. He's in a storm trooper uniform."

"Na man, it's just the regular one."

Josh looks it over, "What the fuck? I got this one at the

theater. It was a special edition I thought. Huh." We think on it for a minute.

One of us says, "Somebody must have taken your figure and switched it for the regular one."

Now I know Trevor works at *Toys 'R' Us,* and has stolen all of his *Star Wars* action figures from there in an attempt to build and maybe someday complete his collection. I pipe up, "You know who I bet it was? Fucking Trevor." Yes, we all agree. Must have been Trevor. Has to have been Trevor. No-one else would have had that much access to Josh's room and also have wanted that stupid fucking action figure that much.

Trevor was a known thief. He'd ask to borrow your lighter then stare at you while he lit his cigarette, waiting to see if you noticed him slipping your cigarette lighter into his pocket. He was always over at Josh and Jeremy's house. He lived just a few blocks away.

We devise a plan to retrieve Josh's figure. This is how it went down: We call Trevor, we go to Trevor's. I bring some weed. We hit the bong on the side of the garage as always. After we're stoned Josh goes into the house to take a shit. I engage Trevor in conversation, try to keep him outside by the garage. Josh searches Trevor's room. Trevor starts to get suspicious, "Man, Josh has been in there for a while."

"Ah man he's just taking a dump," I can see it in his eyes, Trevor's getting restless. He's eying the front door to his house.

Josh walks out the front door, *Skywalker Storm Trooper* in hand, throws it on Trevor's lap. "You motherfucker. I knew it was you." Later on, Trevor would complain to me that I had sold him out on this venture. Fucking Trevor. His reputation would continue to haunt him in later years.

There was an incident at my parent's cabin while my old band *Gris Gris* was recording there. We lived in that cabin from January to March of 04'. Most of the old League City crew showed up at one time or another to visit. Chad suspected Trevor of stealing a bottle of *Jack Daniels* from him. Trevor had been over at Chad and Megan's place earlier in the week. They drank, Trevor left, Chad went to bed and the next morning the bottle was gone. Then fast forward to the weekend and they are both at the cabin. Lars makes a campfire. At some point in the evening Trevor pulls a bottle of *Jack* out of his trunk and Chad, in his Chad way, begins to go off on him. "I knew it. You stole it. You stole my whiskey."

"What? I didn't steal this. I bought this."

"Nope you stole it. You fucking stole it. You motherfucker."

Nobody ever got to the bottom of that one. Trevor just kept saying, "*Jack Daniels?* That shit is ubiquitous man." We drank whiskey that night anyways so who gives a shit.

We all had a bunch of fun tripping on mushrooms later that evening. We picked them off the cow shit in the pasture. Trevor spent most of his trip looking for his *Zippo*, which was in his fucking pocket the whole time if I remember correctly. The whiskey was never brought up again to my knowledge.

-RIVER PIGGERS-

We'd been to this spot before. We had the perfect campsite waiting for us. It was on the Guadalupe River in Comal County Texas. I wanna say it was the summer of 2001. I drove out there with Trey, Jamie's girlfriend Natalie, and another girl. I can't remember her name. We all crammed into the cab of my pickup truck and after a three hour drive we were at the campground.

We grab the site, we had gotten there early enough. The campsite was up from the river a ways, but it had a fresh water spring in it. This is where we would put the keg.

I think there was at least ten or twelve people en route. Jamie, in his beat up Crown Victoria, with Roadhouse, Vik and Shanelle. Chad, in another car, with Graham and his neighbor across the street Sean. And there was also a bunch of Trey's friends coming, including Joey O'Mahony.

Jamie's car breaks down on highway 71. Roadhouse and Vikram immediately abandon Jamie and Shanelle. They hitchhike the rest of the way. Roadhouse told me Jamie was pissed, but him and Vik didn't give a fuck, they were determined to get to the river.

They're stopped by a cop before they can get a ride. "You boys are aware that hitchhiking is illegal, right?"

Vik, "Well, do you think we could get a ride to the next town then?"

Roadhouse, "Yeah, it's pretty far. Twenty miles or so."

"No I can't do that for you." Cop drives away. Protect and serve my ass.

They keep walking down 71 and finally get picked up

by a trucker named, of course, Tex. Tex is apparently a real character, has a bunch of stories about his honeys on the road and their abilities in the back of a rig. "I got a girl up in Michigan, she could suck water through a wooden leg." Then, "Lot lizards man, hell yeah. All the time." And, "They call her ETV, *The East Texas Virgin*."

One of them has to ride in front and listen to Tex's bullshit while the other gets to ride in the back of the rig. I guess, for the person in front, this gets pretty old pretty quick. Vik and Jeremy make a deal to trade places every time they stop.

Tex drops them at a gas station in San Antonio, that's as far as they get with him. Eventually a good samaritan gives them a ride to the campground from there, about 45 minutes away.

So these two jokers finally show up. We set up a tent or two and start kicking back beers, other people arrive. We go down to swim in the afternoon. First sign of trouble, cops, or as Trey would call them, River Piggers. "Son, I'm going to need to see your ID for that beer."

Me, "I'm in my swim trunks, I don't have my license on me. Come on."

"Well you're gonna have to pour that out then."

"Alright, whatever." I pour out the beer, we swim.

Later that day, back at the campsite. Cops again, "Alright, now we need to see your license." I'm not 21 so they take the keg. All that beer plus the $100 deposit for the shell and tap, gone. Bummer, but we have four or five cases of beer behind the seat in my truck, and a bunch of liquor in my bag. So we're still doing OK at this point. We break out the canned beers. I don't know if anybody really got to drink off that fucking keg. I know we tapped it, but we had to let it sit in the stream for a while to settle.

An hour or so gos by, pigs again, they take the canned beer. But fuck it, we've got liquor. Now we start really getting fucked up. I think I narc-out Jaimie for cheating on Natalie, Roadhouse almost drowns in the river, but Sean saves him, and I called Vik yesterday to see what he remembers about the trip, "I remember being drunk, really drunk."

Back at the campsite we're drinking liquor and the pigs return, but we're on the sly a little bit more now since I got the booze in my bag and we're drinking out of plastic cups. But the cops aren't stupid, well they are fucking stupid, there was probably some real crimes being committed in Comal County that evening, or some poor bastard like Roadhouse drowning in the river. Surely something more worthy of their time than a bunch of kids partying.

I have to go in my bag to get my license out for them again. The cop that's fucking with me sees the bottles of liquor. This time they decide to take more action. "Alright son, you are under arrest."

"This is bullshit," I say. They cuff me and Joey (who doesn't drink) and another kid. I argue with these pigs for a bit, "At least let Joey go, he doesn't even drink. Smell his breath." The cops don't believe in justice, so no response from them. They're calling in backup since we're such an unruly and dangerous group of suburban teenagers. Everybody else with half a brain is trying to distance themselves from the situation so they don't get handcuffed too. Then, enter Roadhouse, who does the exact opposite. He has just returned from a late night dip in the river.

"You fucking pigs can't do this. I know our rights. You're trespassing, we rented this campsite. This is bullshit!" I suppose these two gumshoes only had three pairs of cuffs between them cuz they take the ones off Joey and promptly put them on Jeremy. Now both of us are talking shit to these pigs. We somehow convince them to release kid #3. Then four more cops show up. They take me and Roadhouse over to a picnic table away from our campsite. We keep talking shit, which is probably not the best idea since we are in our swim trunks and flip flops with our hands tied behind our backs.

One of the cops starts writing out our citations. He asks me for my name. I say, "I don't have to tell you my name." He writes me a second ticket for failure to identify myself to a police officer. I give him my name. Eventually the two of us calm down, they write us our tickets, and it's off to county with our dumb-asses.

We're on the road for a good half an hour before we get to the jail. It's out in the middle of nowhere. The only thing around is the bail bondsman across the highway and a bunch of farmland. They take our prints and mugshots, (Which can be found on the web still to this day. Pretty fucked up huh? 18 years later) then it's into the drunk tank for us. There's only one other kid in there and he's royally fucked up. He's talking nonsense and lighting matches in the cell. Crazy motherfucker. We sit in there for hours. It's cold.

They take us out around 6 in the morning and feed us a breakfast hot pocket. "Well I guess if nobody bails you boys out in the next hour we're gonna have to put you in general population."

I was thinking originally we'd stay the night, then see a judge in the morning, and it would just be time served. I didn't think of the possibility of gen-pop. "What do you mean general population?"

"It's a room with a hundred or so other guys. Don't worry, you'll get a bunk."

"I'll take my phone call now."

Ring ring ring, "Mom, me and Jeremy are in jail."

"What? No Ashley has ever been to jail before."

Has to be bullshit, I think. My dad has three brothers who have a million kids, who have a million kids. I can't be the only fuck-up. "Mom, I need you to call the bail bondsman. They're gonna put us in general population if we don't get bailed out soon. We are gonna get fucking raped or something." I guess I had watched too many episodes of *OZ* on *HBO*. My mom throws our bail. We are free. We walk down the highway in our swim trunks and flip flops for a while. The sun comes up and we hitch a ride with some dude in an old sedan. We get back to our campsite and pack up our shit. Time to fuck off back to civilization.

I return to Comal County months later to fight my failure to identify myself charge. The DA threw it out straight away. It wasn't like a real trial or anything. I went into the court room, they called Jeremy's name before mine. Of course he didn't bother to pay his ticket or go to court, he knew it would just disappear into the ether with the rest of his citations across the state. They call my name and I go into a room with the DA. He says I should have fought the MIP too. He would have thrown that out as well. Live and learn I guess. There's another 300 bucks to the police state.

I drove up to Austin after my hearing and stayed with Karen. She was living with Sam and Shana at the time. Shana was shooting dope in her room while Sam did Karate in his. Me and Karen laid around and got drunk and listened to Air. Ended up being a nice little trip in the end I suppose.

-RONNIE THE COWBOY IN SAN FRANCISCO-

Ronnie is truly one of my favorite people on earth. This is Roadhouse's dad. He's a marble mouthed son of a bitch, but I can speak Ronnie. On more than one occasion I remember having to translate for people new to Ronnie's speech patterns. The two of them did a little father son road trip back in, I'm gonna say 03' or 04'. Was a long time ago now. Ronnie drug House to every brothel and strip club on the border from Houston to Tijuana. By the time they headed north to San Francisco Jeremy had gotten a little tired of his old man's antics.

They pull into San Francisco in the evening. They get a room in *The Best Western* at 9th and Harrison. Of course they stayed there. Ronnie's nickname at the strip club back home was Cowboy, because he always wore a cowboy hat. Always.

Roadhouse got his nickname in Austin. He was at our friend Thomas' house partying one night and when he woke up in the morning, he grabbed a beer out of the fridge and pounded it. From then on Thomas called Jeremy Roadhouse, in reference to *The Doors* song. If you are not familiar with it, you have been living under a fucking rock.

Roadhouse used to work for Ronnie at his air conditioning business. There was this time Roadhouse had a low tire on his truck. The only compressed gas around was a tank of freon. So House and his dad fill up the tire with freon. Next thing you know we are at some party huffing freon out of Roadhouse's tire, our mouths covered in black grease.

Jeremy and Ronnie's work week consisted of this: Monday through Thursday they did ventilation work at some chemical plant in Texas City. Fridays they worked at *The Ritz*. A strip club off the freeway halfway to Houston from League City. Many a Friday I'd get a call from House. "Hey man you wanna come down to *The Ritz*? My dad'll get us some beers and there's a free buffet."

Me, "No, no thanks."

"You have to come pick me up. My dad's drunk and he won't let me leave."

"OK, Alright."

"Gregry!" Ronnie would say. "Member that time we'er down at *The Hard Rock* and we almost got a free flight to Vegas. Heh' heh' heh."

Sometimes, when me and Jeremy would be eating our strip club buffet, my old drummer Jaimie's mom would walk by our table. "Oh my God. I can't believe you guys are here. I'm so embarrassed." She'd be totally naked mind you. "Oh Jeremy, you're Cowboy's son? I've known Cowboy for years." Ronnie told us her show stopper was shoving ketchup bottles up her ass. Strange to think that when all this was going on, she was my age now.

Anyways, the two of them are in San Francisco. I drive over from Oakland to meet up with them. Ronnie picks me up in a bear hug, "Gregry, Gregry, let's go down to that ole *Larry Flint's Hustler Club*."

Roadhouse, "Goddammit! I don't wanna go to anymore strip clubs or whore houses with you. It's like being on the road with a fifteen year old boy."

So we go to The Mission to some Mexican bar and start drinkin' beer. Ronnie starts to get a little toasted.

Starts telling me about how he likes his shit dirty in the bedroom, "I mean real dirty. Don't tell Jeremy."

We soon realize that if we just take him to the club he'll buy us some drinks and then just fuck off to go chase pussy. So we go back to the hotel and I look up in the phone book where *The Hustler Club* is and we head to North Beach. We roll into The Hustler Club and Ronnie pays for the three of us. As we're entering the club the door guy tells Ronnie, "Excuse me sir, you'll have to remove your hat."

Ronnie says to him, "I don't take my hat off for nobody. Fuckin' faggot! San Francisco faggot. Fuck you, we're outa here boys."

Earlier in the evening we had accidentally wandered into *The Stud*, a gay bar in San Francisco. Ronnie plops down on a stool and gets ready to order his first beer. Me and Roadhouse look around and quickly notice what is going on here. There were other guys dressed up in cowboy garb in this joint as well, but not exactly Ronnie's kind. We gotta get his dad the fuck out of here. I say to him, "Hey Ronnie let's go to another bar."

Ronnie looks around, "What? Why are we leavin'? This place is cool."

"No...... no it's not Ronnie. Let's get outa here." If we had stayed for a beer God knows what would have happened.

So we can't go to *The Hustler Club* cuz ole Cowboy wont remove his hat. Can't hang at a normal bar cuz I'll have to hear about Ronnie's sex life. So we wonder around North Beach. Plenty of other places to choose from right? And the fucking one we choose doesn't serve alcohol cuz it's all nude or some shit. So me and Roadhouse are stuck there drinking *Coca~Cola* while Ronnie's in the back room negotiating for a blowjob. He decides it's too expensive and eventually we leave. We end up at some regular bar where Ronnie buys us a couple of beers. Then he gets directions to *The Lusty Lady*. A place that has jerk off booths in a circle around a stage. I believe it was a dollar for five minutes.

We all went there on the first *Mirrors* tour back in the summer of 01'. After our gig in San Francisco we ask Oscar (a brand new friend at this point) if he knows where *The Lusty Lady* is. We had just met him the day before mind you. Oscar asks a cop. We get directions. The place had been given a glowing review by Vik after he went there a couple years prior to that for *The Rip Off Rumble*. I spent my dollar and had no urge, at all, to masturbate. Trey was a different story. He kept coming out of the booth to get more ones.

Roadhouse says to the jizz mopper, "You got the worst fucking job on the planet."

Jizz Mopper says to Roadhouse, "Yeah, well you got the worst fucking hobby on the planet."

So Ronnie's at *The Lusty Lady* and me and House finally have a chance to catch up. Roadhouse is moving to Seattle to escape all the cocaine in Houston. His brother lives in Seattle. He's going to move in with him, and Ronnie's going for a visit. We shoot the shit for a while then Ronnie shows back up refreshed. I'm going to guess we drank more and then called it a night somewhere in there. I don't remember getting crazy fucked up with his dad or anything.

Years later Ronnie came through again after Roadhouse had moved to Oakland for good. We met him at a bar near *Jack London Square* in the afternoon. He was drunk. I walk in the bar, "Gregry, where can we find some black girls?" Classic Ronnie, nobody can put their foot in their mouth like a Texan. I look around the bar and it's Ronnie and a bunch of black dudes.

I say to him, "Alright Ronnie let's go."

We take him to *The Kerry House* on Piedmont Ave. No black girls in sight. But some barfly gets Ronnie's room number at the hotel. I think she looked alright actually. I don't know if anything ever came of it. I think Ronnie was too fucked up to give a shit either way at that point. I remember the night ending with Ronnie and my girlfriend Kris yelling at each other. They weren't fighting, they were just yelling shit. That's the last time I saw Ronnie. I hope he comes through again soon.

-BOB & GRIS GRIS-

Bob, Josh , Trevor and Vikram all moved to Tacoma in 2000. Bob had gotten a job at some sort of high end audio company building amplifiers for home stereos. The rest of the guys went with him because they had a band together called *Vegetable F*. They were good, but nothing really happened for them in the great white northwest. Josh worked at a fast food fish restaurant. Bob's job went away when the company went under or something. Vik was up to his old tricks and some new ones, and I don't know what the hell Trevor did. Probably just hung around trying to figure out how he was going to get back to Houston and the first piece of ass he had ever gotten. He finally met a girl like a week before they all moved. Can't blame the guy, I ended up in Oakland for a girl. I moved there in May of 02' for a girl named Lisa. I met her on the first *Mirrors* tour the year before.

Tom, our drummer, booked the tour. It started in Dallas, then to Denver, and then I think the next gig might have been Seattle, which we played with one of Jesse (The Duke) Lortz's old bands, *The Zombie Four*. They were like *The Mummies*, but zombies. Vik had got us that gig and he also got us a gig in Berkeley at the co-op Oscar, Lisa, and a bunch of my future California friends lived in, or had lived in.

Oscar had met Vik in the classic Vikram way. *The Rock 'n' Roll Adventure Kids*, a band Oscar played bass in, did a tour of the northwest in 01'. Vik went to their show in Seattle and decided to quit his job and follow them around on tour for a few days. Oscar and Vik became friends over many drinks and many a Vicodin pill. Vik road with him in his truck for the rest of the tour. So when Tom got a hold of Vik to help with booking, Vik hooked him up with Oscar. Oscar was the event coordinator, or whatever you would call it, for this co-op in Berkeley called *Cloyne*. I would later learn that this co-op was notorious for it's drug use and general population of fuck-ups. We played the co-op, and after the show, Lisa offered to give me a tour of *Cloyne*. We hooked up, I moved to California nine months later. We were together for five years. I'll always love her.

I lived at the co-op with her for the summer of 02', then got my own place in Oakland in the fall. I worked at another *Pearle Vision* out here for a few months, but I wasn't making enough money to survive and my boss was annoying, so I quit. Then I Found a job at *Site for Sore Eyes*. Everyone at that store called me Opie, after Ron Howard in *The Andy Griffith Show*. Some of those people never knew my real name, just Opie.

The owner of the place was some old Jew. Real mean bastard. He'd come into the lab at the Berkeley store on a regular basis just to remind us of how fucking stupid we all were. The store manager there was a great guy. His name was Bill. Bill's dead now, has been for years, and I'm not surprised. He kept booze in the lab and would have me do shots with him during business hours. He gave me weed he grew in his backyard. I heard from other people that worked there, he'd do coke in the lab and shit. Dude was i guess around 50 when I worked there. I think he made it to 60 maybe, but not much past for sure.

The lab manager was a big old black lady, funny as

hell. After the owner would come in to berate us she'd be muttering under her breath, "That motherfucker, I ain't gotta take this shit no more." etc.... I could only take it for three months. I elected to work every Sunday if I got every Saturday off. It was a good fit for my partying. Sunday would be slow and I would be working alone, so who gives a shit if I'm hungover.

"Thank the lord!" My Lab Manager said when I told her I would work Sundays, "If I don't get me some Jesus every Sunday I prolly kill a motherfucker." She was great, beautiful lady.

I also worked at the Chinatown store. That was great cuz the lab was all mine, I worked alone. A fucking dream. That location was run by a mother and son team, and what a team they were. One day a fight broke out on the floor. I peak out of the lab for a second to see what all the commotion was about. The manager's son had gotten into a fight with a customer. The son was some wanna be hood. The mother yells at me when she sees me peering out of the lab, "Come here!" Fuck that, I'm not gettin' my ass whipped for twelve bucks an hour. I slink back into the lab. Later she bitches me out for not helping to "protect the store." Mother and son would come into the lab to fight sometimes. The son would use me as a human shield while yelling fuck you at his mom.

"Fuck me? No fuck you!" as she attacks him, with me between the two of them.

I quit that job on my birthday. I remember that morning, there was a set of lenses that just kept coming out off. I did them over and over but either the curve would be off or there would be bubbles in the lens, always something. All morning the owner of the Berkeley store is talking shit to me. The glasses were for the Chinatown store. I finally get them right. I drive them over to Chinatown Oakland from downtown Berkeley, hand the glasses to my boss there, and tell her I quit. I walked away, turned off my phone and got drunk. The next day I had all these messages from the owner saying shit like, "Be a man and talk to me." I called him and told him where to mail my last check.

Then I worked at the *Oakland Zoo*, where all my co-workers referred to me as G-Smooth, my black name from then on. I liked that job. All my co-workers were black teenagers. Our morning would start with us walking down the hill to get all the kids off the buses. Then we'd walk back through the zoo to the top of the hill to start the rides. One of my co-workers saved me from getting hit by monkey shit one morning. "You gotta watch them niggas' G-Smooth." Word.

It was a great job in some ways, I read a book every couple of days. The whole job was essentially pressing a button and waiting two minutes. The rides stopped on their own. So I'd strap the kids in, hit the button and then read. I loved it. Getting paid to read. There was really nothing to do other than that, except for staring off into space, which is what everybody else did. They'd come up to me and ask me, "What you doin' readin' all those books for? You don't talk a lot. You must smoke a lotta bud G-Smooth." I'm reading cuz this job is fucking boring dude. How can you not, smart phones don't even exist at this point.

After a few months my boss has a little talk with me about reading on the job. Apparently it was a safety hazard. I ignore his fat ass and keep reading. I read fucking *Naked Lunch* there. I remember moms always coming up to me and asking me what I was reading. Glad none of them had ever read *Naked Lunch*. I wish I hadn't. I try to conceal my reading for a while, but I keep getting caught, so I stop coming to work.

Then I get a job at *Lens Crafters*. I have that job for five years or so. This one was cool. I remember both the store manager and lab manager telling me at the end of my interview that I would have to take a drug test. I could do it that day or next week or the week after that, but I would have to do it before I started working. Never made good friends at *Lens Crafters*, but nobody fucked with me and I didn't need anymore friends.

After I was settled in California and had some paid time off from *Lens Crafters*, I drove up to Tacoma where Bob and the rest of the guys were then living. It was in 03' sometime. Vik was hooked on Junk, Trevor had moved back to Houston for a girl named Houston, Bob was homeless and Josh hated Bob because Bob fucked his girlfriend. I ran into Bob first, which meant I would barely see Josh. That also meant I was stuck with Bob without a place to stay. The people who he was crashing with were tired of his shit. So we found ourselves aimlessly driving around Tacoma killing time. That was OK though, we had plenty of catching up to do.

One of the days I was there we went to a park on The Puget Sound for a hike. We brought a six pack of beer and a pint of whiskey for the journey. We went out in the woods, smoked a joint, and started getting drunk. After an hour or so I felt a little knock in my guts, "Man, I think I need to take a shit."

Bob, "Fuck, me too."

"Alright, let's see what we got to wipe with." We had the paper bag the whiskey came in and the receipt for the beer. We divide them up and go our separate ways into the forest. We meet back up at the trail just in time for someone with a dog to pass us. We say hello. I remember the guy having a lot of trouble getting his dog out of the woods and back onto the trail. You couldn't blame the dog, that shit was fresh.

Bob was a senior when I was a freshman in high school, he's the same age as my sister. He had a band, *The Illnesses*. They were a punk band, a punk rock 'n' roll band. I'd never heard anything like it.

Bob was almost single handedly responsible for the personality defects in me and over half our friends. He used language you could never use in polite company. The words faggot and cock sucker dripped off our tongues like pussy juice off Ron Jeremy's dick. He used that language anywhere and everywhere, and to anyone and everyone, especially if he was drunk. And I'm not talking about your run of the mill fucking with somebody. This dude could make a motherfucker cry or incite violence with a single tongue lashing. He was the kind of person that would keep you up at night in bed, running scenarios in your brain about what you would say to him the next time you saw him. Or twisted fantasies about beating him to death with a baseball bat. He could talk shit and talk shit he did. Better than anybody I've met since or before. He thickened all of our skins.

And this was exactly why I wanted him to be the new

drummer in *Gris Gris*. Oscar and Lars had become a voting block. Anything that was up for debate, Lars gave his opinion and Oscar seconded that opinion. I needed a fourth member that would not only vote with me, but would make their lives miserable and create a balance of power that would lead to compromise from then on.

Joe had quit the band earlier that year. We did one full US tour with him after *The Gris Gris* self titled LP came out. Then he decided touring wasn't for him. He, at the time, didn't want to be away from Oakland for a third to half the year, which was how life was from 04' to 07'. Always on the road.

Our next victim was Emily. She was drummer number two. We did one tour with her. She was good, certainly better than Bob. Bob wasn't a drummer, he was barely a guitar player. I guess her and Lars and Oscar didn't get along. I got along with her just fine. After the tour Lars and Oscar put their foot down and we kicked her out of the band. What could I do? I was outvoted.

Bob had been kind of following us around on that tour. He was going to massage school at the time and in between sessions in New Mexico, he was back in League City living with his parents just hanging out. He came to all of our gigs in Texas when we came through on tour in 04', and being the charming, fun loving guy he was, ingratiated himself to the rest of the band. After we kicked Emily out of the band, the first person I thought of was Bob. I knew we didn't need a traditional drummer with our set up and I didn't really want one. Plus Bob is one of my best friends and it would be fun to travel the states with another League City fool. So I ask the other guys, "How bout we get Bob to play drums?"

They loved that motherfucker at this point, "Yeah, Bob's cool. Sounds good."

First thing on the agenda was recording *Gris Gris* record number two. My master plan was to take the advance money from *Birdman Records* and live off of it out in the middle of nowhere. I could write the record over the course of three months and then we could put it on tape at the end.

So we end up living at my parent's cabin in central Texas from January to March of 05'. Me and Oscar pack all the equipment, amps, drums, tape machine, mics, keyboards and guitars into a minivan we rented, and drive it to Texas.

Bob and Lars show up a few days later. Lars flies into DFW and Bob grabs him at the airport on his way to the cabin from Santa Fe. Bob is coming later because of his school, Lars is coming later because he had to get surgery.......on his dick!

The two of them show up and of course Bob immediately brings up what is on all of our minds, but nobody else has the balls to ask. (Or maybe we just had the tact to know better, but this is why I love Bob.) "Let's see it Lars. Post-op. Let's see your dick. How was that shit, painful?" Lars without any look of emotion or trepidation undoes his pants and pulls out his cock. Black stitches run up the shaft to the head. I take a peak and quickly look away. Damn that is some shit. Adult circumcision, fuck. Lars doesn't really comment.

The cabin has two floors. Two big rooms essentially. Me and Bob take the upstairs, Lars and Oscar the downstairs. This works out well. Me and Bob wake early, Lars and Oscar late. They stay up all night listening to metal, Me and Bob get stoned and wonder the forest in the morning. What the hell is the point of being nocturnal when you are not only isolated, but in nature too? Beats me.

The months go by, Bob is back and forth from Santa Fe and the cabin. Me and the other three spend the weekends between Houston and Austin. Lots of good times. When we are all at the cabin we work on music a little. Definitely less than we could have. Mostly we just drink and hang out watching the carnage that is the fly tape we hung by the porch light outside. Hundreds of bugs just stuck to this thin strip of plastic eating each other. It was hours of entertainment.

Bob invents a game where Lars runs between two trees while he shoots him with an air pistol. Bob also needs bodies to practice his massage skills on. Oscar and Lars are happy to oblige, fools. I would see the two of them limping around from time to time holding their backs. I told them not to let that motherfucker touch them. I never did. I got drunk one day at the cabin and I twisted my ankle or something. I remember having to hide my injury around Bob. I'd limp in private and when I saw him, for the next week or so, I'd bite my lip and try to walk straight so he wouldn't offer assistance. He caught me once, "Hey what's wrong? You're limping. You want me to take a look?"

"No, I'm good. I'm not limping."

I write a whole bunch of songs at the cabin and at the end we record them, it all works out. We do *South By*

Southwest in Austin back when it wasn't a total nightmare, and then start our US tour.

Jackson, MS is day one of our adventure. Don't remember the show, but I remember the girls me and Bob met. Bob was hooked, the tour starts on a good foot for the two of us. I think everything probably went pretty smooth on tour number one. Bob hasn't gone too overboard on being Bob around Lars and Oscar yet. The, I'm gonna talk shit to everyone 24/7, I don't give two fucks, and you can suck my dick Bob that I will always love and cherish. You know, real Bob. I think tour number two or three is where Bob starts referring to Oscar as "Faggito" cuz he's a pussy. Bob starts being himself eventually and does things like this, for example:

One day, on a long drive, Bob is looking at some porn we bought at a jack shack and decides he just can't take it anymore. With me to his right, and Roadhouse to his left, he puts his coat over his lap and begins to pleasure himself. Both me and Roadhouse know better than to take notice, let alone say anything. I don't remember if he finished or not, but I do recall Roadhouse complaining that Bob was elbowing him in the ribs the whole time he was jerking off. Bob is left handed. Now I'm not saying that none of us except Bob masturbated on tour, but at least we had the common decency to do it in the shower of whoever's house we stayed at.

We took Bob to New York City for his first time, and a bunch of other terrible places on the eastern seaboard. It's funny, when you're in a low level garage band, you don't see nice America, and fuck nice America anyways. You see every shit-hole ghetto from sea to shining sea. Every bar you play at is located in just the worst part of town, and you're so tired and hungover every day you don't have the energy to see the nice things a city has to offer. You've already used all your strength and energy getting from point A to point B, then you have to eat, sound check, and try to get drunk enough to get on stage and do it all over again. Maybe there's a party after the show, maybe there's cocaine, maybe you get a piece of ass. That was always really the end game. Do all this bullshit and just hope that you get laid at the end of the night. I think Lars might have had the strongest game. Sit at the end of the bar alone, be tall, and don't say shit. Seemed to work like a charm.

This is how strong Lars' game was: He went on a blind date once while he was in college. I don't know how it was set up. Not through the internet. The plan for the date was Lars and this girl were gonna go grocery shopping together and then make dinner over at her place. Lars gets royally fucked up the night before, so he's still good and hungover well into the evening when he's supposed to meet up with his date. He goes through with it regardless. Lars is a trooper.

His date picks him up and they head to *Safeway* to get groceries for their dinner. Lars is in bad shape, his stomach is all fucked up and his head hurts, but him and his date are getting along swimmingly. He told me they were walking around the store getting meat and bread, etc........ whatever the fuck, when he feels a fart welling up in his bowels. He tells his date he's going to grab an item that he knows is located on the opposite side of the store, and he'll meet her at the register. He walks off to a distant isle and lets it rip. Turns out it wasn't only gas that escaped from his body in that store. Yes my friends, it was a shart.

Lars panics, what the fuck can he do? He's got shit in his drawers and it's starting to run down his leg. Luckily he's in the back corner of the supermarket near the deli counter, which is closed already cuz it's late. He jumps over the counter, pulls off his pants and underwear, throws his boxers into the trash, and starts to clean his ass with a rag he finds back there. After he has fixed himself up he heads for the front of the store and his date. She motions to him and asks, "What took you so long?"

"Oh, I don't know......" Lars said while they were waiting in line to get rung up he kind of kept his distance from home-girl because he thought he might smell like shit or something. Finally they purchase their groceries and get back into the car.

Lars' date, "What is going on with you? What happened in the store? Why are you acting so strange all of a sudden?"

Lars, "Hmm...... Well, I gotta level with you OK. While we were in *Safeway*, I shit myself." I fucking love Lars, he's certainly an honest man if nothing else. The date continues, they go to her place, make dinner, have sex, and then afterwards she tells him she doesn't mind that he shit himself in *Safeway*. It makes him more real to her. Fucking Lars........ "The Siberian Tickler". And on top of all that he says the next day he woke up with this crazy rash from his balls, across his taint, to his asshole, and down his thighs. The rag he used to clean himself with had bleach on it or something.

Now none of that shit would have ever worked for me. I think I might have even cock-blocked myself a few times running my stupid fucking mouth. But we all got ours here and there after a while. Once you've done the loop around the country a dozen or so times, you have lady friends in enough places that you lose the urge to kill everyone else in the band. It pacifies you, and then if you're good enough at it, it starts to disgust you. *Gris Gris* was once called, "A band of broke, roaming, alcoholics that are too brain dead to realize that psychedelia was fucking dumb." And maybe we were that, but we fucking jammed. Maybe not so much with Bob in the band, but we still had our moments, and people liked the show even if we played like shit. The way we set up made us such a freak show or anomaly that no matter what, people enjoyed it. People wanna see something different, not just the same guitar, bass and drums playing rock 'n' roll with the vocals so lost in the over-amped guitars that all you really hear is a set of extremely boring instrumental music.

We did a few tours with Bob. We never let him drive. We did once, and that was enough. He tried to use the cruise control in The Rocky Mountains. That was the first and last time. At a stop along the way, the three of us had a huddle while Bob was in the shitter.

Lars, "We can't let Bob drive anymore."

Me, "Agreed."

Oscar, "Yeah, he's crazy. Fuckin' asshole." Bob comes back to the van.

Lars, "Let me have the keys, I'm gonna drive for a bit."

Bob, "What the fuck? I've only been driving for twenty minutes."

Me, "Yeah, let somebody else drive."

Bob, "Fuck you. Fuck all you guys. You don't see me

complaining when you guys are hungover as shit everyday behind the wheel." We get back into the van and Lars drives. Carefully and slowly like you should through the mountains in a piece of shit minivan that is carrying way more weight than it was designed to.

Me and Bob have definitely been through some shit together in our day, that's for sure. We've shared a couple near death experiences. One involved a fire in my apartment in Oakland. It was the summer and Bob was staying with me and Lisa. We lived in a studio of course, so one room for the three of us. Quaint.

We were between tours and Bob was kind of homeless and in limbo. He sort of lived with his parents in League City, but really lived on the road or in his minivan. It was hot that summer, and I always kept a box fan in the back doorway to keep a breeze going through the apartment. The fan took a shit at some point, and I was too broke to buy a new one, so I took the thing apart and attempted to repair it. I found that a mass of dog hair had gummed up the motor. Lisa had an adorable little puppy named Toki. The little monster ate my wallet ruining my driver's license, chewed up my shoes, and fucking barked constantly at nothing. She was an obnoxious little devil, very cute though. Toki was a Shih Tzu-Maltese mix, a Chinese lap dog. I kind of hated Toki.

So I clean out the dog hair and decide I'll lubricate the motor with 10W-30. I didn't have any WD-40, but I did have motor oil for my car. I figure that's a motor, this is a motor, what's the difference? I reassemble the fan and it works like a charm. Lisa leaves town that day to visit her folks or something, so me and Bob have the place to ourselves. Of course we go out and get shit-face drunk.

We come home sometime late at night all fucked up. I pull open the sliding door to the backyard, click on the fan and immediately pass out. Bob does the same. Him on the couch, me on the mattress on the floor. Real swanky place we had, let me tell you.

At some point in the night I am woken by Bob. He is screaming at me, "THE FUCKING DRAPES ARE ON FIRE, WAKE THE FUCK UP!" The whole apartment is filled with black smoke. The drapes are in fact on fire, and the fan is melting into itself. A ball of fire is emanating from it's motor, melting the plastic blades. We tear the drapes down and throw them into the yard. I kick the fan out the door. We douse all that shit with water, the fire is out. Luckily the drapes didn't catch the wall on fire or something.

Bob tells me he was sleeping and Toki was just freaking out, barking and jumping on him and scratching his face. She saved our lives. If Toki had not been there, me and Bob would surely have died of asphyxiation. The apartment was full of toxic black smoke. Produced, I'm guessing, from a combination of 10W-30, fan plastic, and polyester drapes being incinerated. Before the place burned down we would have suffocated.

Now, I suppose I could look at this in two ways. Had Toki not woken Bob up, we would have both died. But, had Toki not been around in the first place, the fan wouldn't have gotten gummed up with her hair, and my dumb ass wouldn't have lubricated the thing with motor oil. Either way this began my love affair with little Toki. I started to sleep with her cradled in my arms. I no longer cared where she chose to shit and piss, what she destroyed or how much she barked. She was now my little angel.

Toki died this last summer. She made it to 14 or 15, I lost track. Me and Lisa broke up years ago, but we have always stayed in touch. Sometimes when I'd be down in LA, I'd end up at Lisa's, and get to see my little gremlin. Lisa is now a veterinarian, so Toki always had top-notch health care. I think some cancer or something finally did her in. Lisa told me, in the end, she had to euthanize Toki. She did it in her apartment in Hollywood. Another person from her clinic helped her inject Toki with whatever they use. As Lisa held Toki in her arms, she said she saw the life go out of her eyes. She said it was a very peaceful death. God bless you Toki, you little monster. I'll see you in the void, licky no bitee.........

I wish I had a better end to this story, but I don't. One day Joe decided he wanted back into the band and we kicked Bob out. No argument between the three of us. I had gotten my fill of watching Bob torture Oscar and Lars, and they had gotten their fill too. Now, it may seem like I'm talking shit here, or that I'm a sick sadistic fuck, but I really love Bob. I don't think I'd make the music, or be the person I am, for better or worse, without having known him. He turned me, and all our friends, on to 77' punk and San Francisco garage rock. Music no other kids in the suburbs back then were getting their hands on. I looked up to the guy. He made it apparent by example of what was possible. He would rent out *The Elk's Lodge* down in Kemah and have punk bands from Austin play there. A fucking *Elk's Lodge* in the suburbs south of Houston. We were surrounded by nothing but strip malls and hillbillies.

Nobody knew what the fuck to make of us, even the kids at our own school. While they played in their lame *Green Day* cover bands and shopped at *Hot Topic*, we were getting drunk and listening to *The Mummies* and *The Pack*, all while huffing freon out of our parents air conditioning units and saying, "Fuck your bland suburban culture League City, you can kiss my ass."

-A JOHN BROTHERS BAR FIGHT-

Back in the spring of 2014 I took *The John Brothers Piano Company* on tour. None of these guys had ever toured before. They are all around seven or eight years younger than me. I thought it was time these boys saw every shit hole ghetto in America, got drunk in that ghetto, and really experienced what it's like to live like a total dirt-bag for a month or so.

They're all from California and have no idea of what a dump the rest of the country is. I took them in the spring. I'll only tour in the spring or fall. The weather sucks everywhere else in America the rest of the year. So they had a somewhat skewed vision of what the places we stopped in were really like. I couldn't last a summer or a winter anywhere east of Oakland at this point, and I've only been here 17 years. These pussies grew up on the west coast, they wouldn't last a week. Every city we stopped in they'd say, "Man we should move here, it's so cheap." Wait till the season changes fuckers........

Anyways, I started playing bass for them a couple years prior to this. I really have no business playing bass in a jazz band. I once passed out drunk, at *The Monterey Jazz Festival*, on Bobby Hutherson, the legendary vibraphone player. I didn't realize who i had slept on until I looked at the credits of Eric Dolphy's *"Out to Lunch"* record one day, or actually Arlo did. "Hey Greg check out who you passed out on." He shows me the LP.

Me being in the band was all an accident. It seems like all the projects I've been in since I moved to California have been accidents. When I moved to Oakland from

Texas I remember specifically saying to myself, "Never be in a band again. Too much bullshit." Of course that wasn't what ended up happening.

Gris Gris became a band because, when I moved to California, Oscar kept bugging me about playing bass. And he's a good bass player, so I gave in. Then he said, "Hey, we should get Joe to play drums for us." So I think OK, but just two drums.

Then there was Lars. He was Oscar's house-mate. When my first solo record came out, I wanted to re-create the record live. I saw an electric piano at Oscar's one day. I asked, "Who's electric piano is this?" Oscar told me it belonged to Lars. I asked Lars, "You play piano?"

"I took lessons when I was a kid, but I haven't played in ten or fifteen years." He picked it back up no problem, and all of a sudden Lars was in the group too.

I recorded my friend Eric Johnson in January or February of 08'. His stage name is *Sir Lord Von Raven*, which would become the name of the band. (Also known as *SLVR*) Like *Alice Cooper* or something. I recorded him at my studio and played the bass and lead guitar. Jay Bronzini, who would become a close friend, played the drums. After we finished the record and it came out, Eric wanted to re-create the record live. So we got a bass player, Josh Miller, and we did a live show with the four of us. Next thing you know I'm in that band for seven or eight years. By far the longest run I've had in any band in my life.

The John Brothers Piano Company was the biggest accident of all. John and Thatcher moved into the warehouse I lived in in 2011. They had both just finished college at *UC Berkeley*. John with an English degree and Thatcher with a degree in mathematics. Their room at the warehouse was only $500 for the two of them, but after the first month they couldn't come up with the rent. You'd think one of them could have gotten a job with their credentials, but neither of them bothered. Damon, the guy who ran *The Ghost-town Gallery* and held the lease, was livid. He threatens to kick them out. They brainstorm. "What can we do to make rent?" One of them comes up with the idea to move their spinet piano out onto the street in San Fransisco and busk. They both are great piano players and write their own music. They made rent in two days and that's how it all started. The two of them just trading off on the piano. They played parties for the rich, parties for internet companies, house parties, parties for a flamboyant realtor, weddings, a bunch of shit. They were savvy business men, and they knew how to get paid. Money was always contentious between the two of them. They argued like brothers over every insignificant thing you could think of.

The first thing I did with them musically was to record them. We did this, the first time, at the warehouse. There act at this point in time was just them trading off on piano, and it was great. The piano I had upstairs in my studio was not as good as the piano downstairs in the practice room, so I ran a long microphone cable out my window and down through the skylight into the practice space. I didn't feel like running a headphone extension that far and they didn't really need headphones anyways, so communication was limited. I could hear what was going on in the practice room downstairs from my bedroom upstairs, but whoever was downstairs had no way of knowing what was going on upstairs. I used one condenser mic a few feet away from the piano to record them. I figured this would be the best way to capture what I had seen them do live at house parties and warehouse parties before.

John went first. I told him, "Just say the name of each song before you play it and then say stop when the piece is done."

He heads downstairs, Thatcher hangs in my room with me. John plays five or six tunes and then says, "OK, I'm done." He comes back upstairs. Now it's Thatcher's turn, he heads down. Me and John hang in my room. Remember, we can hear everything that is happening in the practice room due to the fact that I'm using a condenser, or "room mic" to record the piano. Thatcher begins, and it's beautiful and all of that. Me and John just sit there, each drinking a 24 of *Foster's*, listening to this serene piano music in the midday haze of cigarette smoke in my room.

He gets through three or four songs and then we hear the door to the practice room slide open. It's loud, the door is heavy like an old industrial freezer door. I think that room might have been some sort of refrigeration chamber for the place back in the day when it was still a creamery. It's Damon, "What's going on Thatcher?"

"Hey Damon."

"You guys had a bar b que last week, up on the roof?"

"Uh.......yes."

"Alright, I'm not doing you guys' dishes anymore."

"Uh, well Maria did, we did all the dishes from tha-"

"Naaah, I watched after the bar b que, they're still

sittin' up there. You got the grill with the spatula even on it."

"I-I had to go, I did a ton of dishes up there. I told John to do the rest." Thatcher is attempting to deflect Damon's anger towards his room mate. I love it!

Damon again, "My man, I just, you guys, we're not even making rent in this building. I'm too busy to start, I can't even rent upstairs because it's a shit-hole. The bathroom's shit, the kitchen's shit. I show the building. You know what? We have two open rooms, we're not even making our rent. We haven't paid rent because it's a shit-hole up there. Not once have you guys helped out. We missed the trash too...... John has started."

At this point me and John are on the floor fucking cracking up. He is tearing Thatcher a new asshole and we get to be the fly on the wall for the whole thing. I had heard some of these chew out sessions before through the walls of my room. They're fucking hilarious! Luckily I've never had one directed towards me. I just avoid his ass when I can tell Damon is in one of his moods. First person he sees he just lays into and blames everything on them.

Damon continues, "I love that you love our practice room and everything, but we're not making enough money on our house. I'm not kiddin'. You guys, you're just fucking it up for everybody. I'm talking about you, and a hundred other people. I'm bitchin' at you, then I'm gonna go bitch at Tony, then I'm gonna bitch at everybody up there. AJ who left dishes. You guys gotta stop, I can't rent these rooms. They come in the kitchen, it's a fucking health hazard dude."

Thatcher, "All's I'm sayin' is that me and Maria did

every single dish in that kitchen before we left man."

Damon, "All's I'm sayin' is, from here on out, if I catch you guys leaving dishes up there and not-and by the way, the bathroom looks like shit. I just fucking cleaned it for everybody. We all shit in there dude. I'm just lettin' you know....... I'm at the end of my line. I can't rent this house. You know we-I pay for all you guys to be able to have all this practice space. I don't have time to fucking clean this bitch, or play my music in here because of you guys. John has stepped up."

Me to John, "Shit he loves you John."

Damon, "However, I saw you guys' plates in there and I washed em. I'm not gonna clean them anymore. They're still sitting up there, so is the bar b que spatula you guys used."

This shit is totally scatter shot at this point, Damon is in full psycho mode. "So is all the trash out there that AJ cleaned up for you by the way. All the litter, all the trash that blew over from the bar b que spilling over, all the beer cans, all your recycling up there, everyone of those beers I watched you guys drink. You don't take that shit out. Sorry buddy, I'm about-when I put a pink slip under the door I'm taking everybody's fucking keys. Go find a new place. John's cool."

Both me and John, "Ha ha, fuck, oh shit, ha!!!!"

Damon, "I didn't rent this place to you and your friends. I don't know your friends. I mean why don't you just fucking help out? You didn't take out the trash when I asked you to help us out that week......"

Thatcher, "I'm tryin' man, I'm tryin'."

John to me, "Oh shit, Thatcher is groveling like a little

bitch!"

Damon, "That's cool just go find yourself another place, get your pianos out. Cuz obviously you're mad instead of going, yeah I'll help out."

Thatcher, "I tried to man, when I was over here, I tried to do....... uh I'm tryin' man."

Damon, "You know what man, instead of being like hey Damon, you're right, I do admit some-"

Thatcher, "Look I-I-I know you're right I'm just telling you, I know you're right and I gotta do more, but I'm just tellin' you, I'm tryin', I am, you know I'm not-"

Damon, "Well next month if it's continued I'll just take your keys and you can find a new place to live. Enjoy." Door slides open and shut again.

Thatcher, "I'm coming up." Classic, we used this for the secret track on the CD they made later.

Fast forward a couple years, Ive become friends with them. Thatcher has dusted off his clarinet from when he was a kid, and they want to put together a band. I told them I could play bass until they found somebody else. I loved the kind of ragtime, stride piano jazz they were playing. I loved playing bass and I figured I could fake it for a little while. It would be something fun to do for a couple months. Next thing you know I'm in the group for four years. Jimi enters the group on drums and Arlo on trumpet. They both went to college with the Johns.

So now I'm getting ready to record *Another Generation of Slaves* and I think, "Who better to be the backing band than these guys?" They play on the record, we do shows around the bay, and then I decide I wanna do a tour to promote the record. I get Scott Winland to book it.

I take them on the road for a month. We do a set of my stuff and a set of the jazz stuff each night. We fly to Austin with as much gear as we can take on the flight. We rent a suburban in Austin and buy a piano in Arkansas. Our first gig is in Chicago. After the show Arlo complains, "Man Jimi is already getting laid. It's the first gig of tour, shit."

I say, "Arlo, we're all gonna get laid on this tour. Trust me."

We tour around the Midwest and Canada. We go to New York, Boston and Philadelphia. All the places on the east coast I could give two shits about. Thatcher is missing one of his front teeth. We start calling him "Kentucky John Thatcher". His smile is endlessly entertaining, especially when he has to take out his fake tooth to play the clarinet.

We play The Blackout Fest in Athens, OH. We're there for four days I think. The last night we are in town we go to yet another of many parties on this tour. Jimi takes acid, Thatcher stays up doing coke, and I get loaded. I think I might have passed out drunk for an hour or so on the floor before somebody started blaring *The Dead Milkmen* and woke me up. Thatcher has something goin' with this girl that is also a coke fiend. He doesn't like her, but he likes her cocaine. As we are leaving town she follows him back to the fleabag motel we got but barely stayed in. He tell's me, "Let's get the fuck out of here." I think it might have been Easter that day. We ate at *KFC*. Man I felt like death. *KFC* didn't help either.

After that Thatcher is transformed from "Kentucky John Thatcher" to "Cheddar Jack" because for like the next three days those are the only two words he seems to be able to utter. His lips are swelled to twice their size and he is just fucking retarded. All he can do is eat *Cheddar Jack Cheese-its* and play clarinet. Works for me.

After Athens was Cleveland. We played at *The Beachland Tavern*. That's where I usually play in Cleveland, so no surprises there. Show went off without a hitch, not that well attended, but we played good. We stayed at a friend of a friend's place that night. I think we all went to bed pretty early.

In the morning I am loading our bags back into the suburban we rented when I notice one of the bag tags has a foreign last name on it. I'm thinking to myself, "I think I know everyone's last name. Who has a Japanese last name?" I pull all the bags out of the back of the vehicle and realize we have four bags that are not ours. We have been traveling for three weeks, in and out of Canada, down the east coast and then back west with four stranger's bags. Poor bastards, they must have gotten off that plane from Oakland and just been totally screwed.

When we landed in Austin I rushed off with John to pick up the rental and left the other three guys with the responsibility of grabbing all of our checked bags. When I got back to the airport with the rental we were in a rush, so I wasn't paying the closest attention to what we were trying to cram into that suburban. Apparently nobody else was either. Many bags look alike for sure, but check the fucking tags, Jesus. There could have been anything in those bags, and we took them across an international border. The people we stayed with said they would take care of bringing the bags to the airport in Cleveland and making sure they got to their rightful owners. The suburban was a lot easier to load for the rest of the trip, much less Tetris involved.........

After Cleveland was Pittsburgh, but on the way we make a detour to visit our buddy Wallace in prison. He's doing three years for trafficking marijuana, at least that's what I think his charge was. He got pulled over in Philadelphia with a thousand pounds of bud and something like thirty grand in cash. Wallace played sax on a bunch of my stuff, a dear friend. He lived in Oakland, but was on the East Coast doing some of his gangster shit when he got busted.

We all enter the prison, which looks like it was built in the 19th century or something. There's two rows of razor wire fence surrounding the whole place and guard towers at every corner. We go through metal detectors and all that bullshit, then are led into the visiting room. There's families with their kids and mostly, big surprise, a bunch of poor black dudes in brown jump suits. Wallace comes out, we all give him a big hug. We only have about an hour with him because it took us so long to get there, but I know he cherished it. When I got thrown in rehab and Lars and Eric visited me, it was like the best day of my life, and I only stayed in that motherfucker for three days before I checked myself out. Wallace didn't have that option, and he was doing three years.

Nearing the end of the tour we find ourselves in New Orleans. We play during the day on the street in front of a hat shop that one of Arlo's friends from Berkeley works at. We make 400 bucks in 30 minutes. The music is exactly what the tourist crowd wants. Later that evening we play the show Scott booked. It's at a place called *Saturn Bar*, another shit hole in the ghetto of course. They give us a couple free beers, but mainly we just drink scotch on the sidewalk out front since you can drink anywhere in New Orleans. At some point someone mentions the owner of the bar is crazy and is weird about shows going late. I'm thinking, "It's New Orleans, some bars never close here, not even for a hurricane."

The bartender was a salty old bitch. I had dealt with her kind before, "You guys are late! You were supposed to be here at nine."

I shrug it off. We're playing last. The PA is shit, it's not like there's gonna be a sound check or anything. The first two acts play, then it's my set. Goes great, then it's *The John Brothers* set. We start to play, and at this point it's not even midnight. Three songs in and the door guy comes and yells in my ear, "Ya'll guys gotta stop, show's over."

I yell, "Alright." Bewildered, I ask, "Well, can we just finish this song?" I know it's a long one.

"OK, but that's it. Owner called."

"OK", I think, "This is fucked." The song goes on and on and on, the door guy is getting impatient. He eventually turns off the PA which doesn't do shit because we are essentially an acoustic act. The trumpet and clarinet are mic-ed up, but you can still hear them fine without the bullshit sound system the club has. It's a small room.

I'm sitting down in the back next to Jimi, as always, and Thatcher is in front. The door guy starts yelling at him from behind the PA. I can't make out what the door guy is trying to say to him but I am pretty sure it's similar to the conversation I just had. I see Thatcher nod his head as dude yells at him, then like Caesar in The Colosseum,

Thatcher gives a thumbs up, then slowly twists his wrist into a big thumbs down. Thatcher goes back to playing his clarinet, the door guy is pissed. The veins on his forehead are starting to pop. He approaches Thatcher and starts yelling more shit at him. "This will be interesting," I think.

Door Guy to Thatcher, "I told you to stop playing right fucking now!"

Thatcher, "Fuck you, get the fuck out of my face."

A bit taken aback by this, the door guy says, "Really?"

Then Thatcher with his toothless shit eating grin, "Yeah...... Fuck you."

The door guy picks him up by the neck and throws him into the drum kit. His clarinet explodes into its different pieces. All hell breaks loose. The opening band is even against us. No solidarity in the music world. Jimi is off the drums in a fist fight with one of the patrons. John has left his piano and starts screaming, "You can't do that to my friend, we're from Oakland!"

Two guys from the opening band jump John. Arlo pulls one of them off him and throws him to the floor. One of Arlo's friends from Austin comments, "This is the best jazz show I've ever been to."

John ends up dragging the other guy into the bathroom. He's beating the shit out of this guy on the piss covered tile floor. The other dude is back and is punching John in the back of the head and pulling his hair. John doesn't seem to notice. Thatcher's yelling at the door guy, saying something about paying for his broken clarinet. I'm hiding in the corner with my bass yelling at everybody, "Just calm down! Stop fighting, everybody just calm down." Some of this, but unfortunately not all of this, is caught on video by a couple that saw us play at the hat shop earlier.

The fight ends eventually. Thatcher is now yelling at the bartender that his clarinet is broken and that he's gonna sue the place. I tell him to shut up. Arlo starts in, and I tell him to shut up too. I'm trying to get our money, and our stuff, and get the fuck out of this place before we all get our asses kicked. I get our forty bucks and then another guy from the bar comes up to me and says, "Sorry about this. It's just that (whatever the door guys' name is) just came out of the closet and your clarinet player called him a faggot." I think, well that's entirely possible. He doesn't look gay or seem gay, but that's entirely possible that Thatcher called him a faggot.

We leave. Thatcher and the other guys in the Suburban, me with Chad from *Wizard Sleeve* (Not Chad from League City). *Wizard Sleeve* Chad lives in Mobile, but is in New Orleans for work. He does construction or something. He came out to see me play but missed it and only caught the bar fight. He thought the show would be later just like everyone else. We finally get to this party at some older woman's house that Arlo's friend from the hat shop is fucking. Her home looks like it came straight out of *Gone With The Wind* or something. It's a proper southern plantation home "servants" quarters and all.

I tell Chad the story the guy at the bar told me. Chad says, "That guy's not gay. I've known him for years." So for some reason, the other guy that works at the bar came up with this elaborate fiction to make me feel like we were somehow responsible for the brawl earlier. Fucking ridiculous. Me and Chad sit around drinking beer and catching up on old times.

After a while, Miss Whoever and homeboy decide they're ready to screw and they kick everyone out. We all walk outside and realize Thatcher is missing. Apparently he had left the party earlier to get down with some chick he met there. I guess it doesn't work out for him so they part ways. Thatcher finds himself lost in New Orleans in the middle of the night with a dead cell phone. He looks for a pay phone, no luck. He stumbles into a landfill where some gutter punks are having a fire in a barrel. One of their faces is covered in blood. Thatcher asks to use one of their cell phones. Thatcher finds out that gutter punks don't have cell phones, at least not back in 2014.

He eventually finds his way back to Miss Whoever's house. Arlo's friend answers the door naked with a hard-on. Thatcher says to him, "I need to use your phone."

Arlo's friend pointing at his dick, "Can't you see I'm busy."

"I don't give a fuck about your dick." Thatcher pushes his way into the house. He gets kicked out. Eventually we run into Thatcher at a gas station where John is buying his second round of fried chicken for the evening. Thatcher is getting kicked out of that place for demanding change in an inappropriate manner. Thatcher's clarinet turns out to be fine. We drive to Houston the next day.

Houston is uneventful except for the fact that Jimi's parents come to the show. They are the greatest couple of Kiwis on the planet. I especially love his mom Pip. "Grig, how you doing? Can I bum a fag off you? I'm not supposed to be smoking. It'll be our little secret." She would come and see us play at *The Boot and Shoe Service* on a regular basis. John was talking about Aderol one time before we played, specifically that he was on it. Pip, "What are you guys tawking about? Iderol? Oh, it's speed? You should give some to Jimi, he's looking a bit tired this evening." Lovely woman that Pip.

Another time I was having dinner over at Jimi's, and in attendance was Jimi, his girlfriend Kala, Pip, and Jimi's brother Sam. I get loaded and tell Jimi in front of everyone, "Jimi, I think I wanna fuck your mom."

Everyone kind of laughed and told me to, "Shut up Greg/Grig."

Anyways, back to the tour. Then it's on to *The Austin Psych-Fest*. We played that. Some of us took drugs, I think I just got drunk. I remember Jimi pissing off the lighting guy cuz he was making shadow puppets in front of his stupid gels or whatever, while some lame "psych band" jerked off on stage.

After Austin we returned the suburban we rented. I had picked up another hand-me-down car in League City from my folks. Me, Arlo, and John drove that back to California and did a few more dates on the way home. Thatcher and Jimi flew back to Oakland from Austin.

Nothing really interesting happened to us in the Southwest. John pointlessly searches for an acoustic piano every night to no avail. He has to play this crappy old *Casio* keyboard for the rest of the trip. Drives him nuts. We drop John off at some mall in the desert outside of LA. His folks live out there and they are gonna pick him up from said mall. John was going to spend a few days at their place before he came back up to The Bay.

So then it's just me and Arlo. We pull into Oakland

before sunset, unload the gear into *The Ghost-town*, and walk down to the liquor store. It's like we never left. As we're walking in, one of the middle easterners that works there is pushing a guy with his pants down out the door. Ah, home sweet home........We sit on the roof of *The Ghost-town* and drink a six pack together. Then I go home and sleep with my wife.

-JAY REATARD-

I was by no means a close friend of Jay Reatard. I'd hang out with him here and there on tour, stayed at his house in Memphis once. I liked the guy. He was fucking nuts. The only real clear memory I have of him is hanging out with him on a tour I did to promote *Painted Garden*. The band I had consisted of me, Brian Glaze, Brad Dunn, and my old band-mate from *The Mirrors*, Alan. We played a kind of musical chairs on stage. We all traded off instruments depending on the song. Half the set was my stuff and the other half was Brad and Brian's.

We played in Memphis and right after the set Jay rushes the stage, "Greg, let's go do some coke."

"Alright just let me get my stuff off the stage real quick."

Jay, "Alright, just hurry up." I hurry, then go into the back stage area. Jay pulls me into a bathroom with a friend of his. A very big friend. The bathroom is tiny. Toilet faces the door and there's a sink attached to the wall. Big guy is by the toilet, Jay's by the door in front of the sink and I'm in between the two. Jay rips the mirror off the wall and sets it on the sink. He chops out three lines. Big guy does his. I eat mine. "What the hell are you doing?" Jay asks me.

"I just eat coke now, been fucking with my nose lately. Works the same, it just comes on slower, but the high lasts longer." I used to drop key bumps into my wine. Great way to do cocaine.

Jay stands there dumbfounded. "That really works?"
Me, "Yeah."

Jay, "You know what I'm gonna do? I'm gonna put it up my ass. You think that'll work?"

"Yeah that'll work. I'm sure of it." (Flashback to the 90s and all the times me and my friends plugged ecstasy.) Jay turns to the liquid soap dispenser on the wall and puts a little bead of soap on his index finger. Then he pulls down his pants, scoops up the coke with his finger and starts working it into his asshole.

He's leaning on me and I'm leaning on the guy behind me. So I'm sandwiched in between these two fuckers in this tiny bathroom and Jay starts moaning, "Ah Greg it burns. Fuck, it burns." He eventually finishes, pulls his finger out of his asshole and puts it directly into his mouth licking it clean. Alright Jay, you win.

Of course I tell this story to everyone I see on the road for like a year or two. The next time I see Jay is at a festival in LA we were both playing at *The Echo*. I see Jay, "Hey man, what's up? How you been?"

"Hi," Jay walks away. I don't know if that story ever got back to him, but he gave me the cold shoulder from that day forward. Then one afternoon, maybe a year later, I was recording a band at my studio in Oakland. Between takes one of the kids in the group looks at his phone and announces to the rest of us that Jay Reatard has died. Huh, I think, wonder how that happened? The guy that liked to give himself wine enemas on stage is dead. It sucks, but I wasn't totally shocked. I suppose it wouldn't have been a big surprise if any of us died from a drug overdose back in those days with the kind of shit we got into. Rest in peace Fucker. If I believed in God maybe we could hang again.

-A BEACH NORTH OF SANTA CRUZ-

It was a weekday. Don't ask me which one. I woke up drunk at the old church I now live in. I didn't have anybody to record that day, or for that matter, the whole week. I hadn't been working very much at this time. I decided I wanted to get out of the ghetto for a night or two. So I pack up a little food and some clothes and bedding and hit the road for this camp spot I go to just north of Santa Cruz. I head down the 880 going south. Somehow I miss The San Mateo Bridge to get over to Half Moon Bay to hit the Pacific Coast Highway. I realize this, at some point, just north of San Jose. I stop at some strip mall to get directions. Maybe there's another way to get over to the 1 without having to go through the hell that is San Jose, and the other hell of driving west on the 17 through the mountains. Then I'd have to go through Santa Cruz and drive back north on the 1 to get to where I want to camp. It's a beautiful spot full of cypress trees right above the beach. You can camp under the trees and you don't even really need a tent or anything. They make the perfect covering. You can camp there illegally for free. The spot is owned by some lumber company or something. It says keep out, no camping, no fires, etc..... probably mostly for legal reasons of liability, but they obviously don't give a shit if you camp there because next to the keep out signs there was once another sign that said, "Log onto this website to tell us your stories of camping here." I'm not gonna specify where the spot is cuz I don't want a bunch of you fuckers going there and ruining it for the rest of us in the know.

Anyways, I'm in a strip mall parking lot with a *Chipotle* and some other chain stores. I try to approach people for directions. I didn't think I looked that fucking crazy, but the people in the parking lot repeatedly ignore me, jump in their cars and lock their doors. Fucking Californians.

One time I sold a guitar pedal on *Craigslist* to a chick in San Jose and she paid me extra to bring the pedal to her because she was afraid to come to Oakland. I did that and my alternator went out on the way home. I parked my piece of shit car on the side of the interstate and walked to the nearest BART station, returned the next day with a new alternator, and finally got my car home. I lost money on that sale to say the least.

So none of these fuckers in the parking lot are gonna help my ass, so I go into *Chipotle*, something no human being should ever do to themselves. I talk to one of the employees. "Man I've been trying to get directions from people in the parking lot and no-one will talk to me. Do I look like a crazy person?" He shrugs and gives me the bad news that yes I'll have to either go back north to hit The San Mateo Bridge or go south through San Jose to cross the mountains to Santa Cruz.

So I drive through the fucking mountains, stop in Santa Cruz to buy an 18 pack of Coors Light and probably some snacks or some shit. I hit the 1 north and finally get to my spot midday. Great! I fucking made it. I plop down under a tree with a cold one and my guitar and start doin' my thing. I drink and sing and read a bit. The day wears on, I take a walk down the beach. I see the usual random blue hair yuppie jogger lady, some surfer bros, and the forests of kelp and other random sea junk that have washed up onto the shore. It's a beautiful day of course, and I'm getting drunk as hell.

Now for the gap my friends. I'm hangin' on the beach, I'm under the trees, I'm playing my guitar watching the sunset, and then........I black out. I come to and it's night time. I'm climbing through some bushes up an embankment, lost and confused as hell. A light is being shined in my eyes. I say, "Ah, get that fucking light out of my eyes. What the fuck?"

Random guy with a flashlight, "Where are you coming from?"

"I'm camping down by the beach."

"How the hell did you get out here?"

"I drove."

"Where's your car?"

"My trucks parked right over there."

"I don't see any truck."

"No? It's somewhere around here." I'm pretty much out of ideas at this point. I'm Standing on the Pacific Coast Highway in the middle of the night with some random stranger with a flashlight asking me questions. My truck is nowhere to be seen. And when I look back at where I came out of, it ain't the fucking cypress grove shit that I always camp at. What the hell is going on?

Random guy again, "I don't know, you seem pretty confused and drunk. You think your truck is at one of the other turnouts? And I hate to tell you this pal, but you only have one shoe on."

I look down, sure enough, white shoe on one foot. Other foot, just a tattered sock. Damn. "Man, could you drive me down to the next turnout or something? Help me find my truck."

"Uh I don't think I wanna let you in my car."

"Please, I'm begging you, it's the middle of the night. I'm lost and drunk and just totally confused."

"I'll tell you what. I'll drive up to the next turnout and see if your truck is there."

"Thank you so much. It's a 1985 Dodge Ram with a camper shell. It's red, you can't miss it."

"OK, I'll be back in a minute." He drives off. I stand on the side of the highway in the moonlight freezing with my one shoe.

Eventually homeboy returns. "I didn't see your truck up there and I need to get goin'. I don't know what to tell you pal."

"Please could you drive to the turnout north of here and see if it's there? I'm begging you, I'm stuck."

"Alright, OK. I guess I can do that."

"Thank you so much." He drives off into the night once again. I wait and shiver. 20 minutes or so go by. He returns.

"I found your truck it's at the next turnout, so good luck."

"Oh thank god. Can you please give me a ride there?" "Uh I don't know, there's not much room in my car and I really need to get going." His car is full of random shit like he's moving or something and there's a case of bottled water in the front seat. The back seat is packed to the gills with all of his belongings.

"Please give me a ride. It's the middle of the night, it's freezing, and like you said, I only got one shoe. Also walking down this narrow winding highway right now is totally insane." My foot without the shoe is already raw and the sock is worn through.

"Alright, I'll do it. I knew another guy from Texas (he saw the plates on my truck) that drank too much and well, he was a good guy actually, so I'll help you out I guess." Thank fucking God! We rearrange some of the shit in the front seat, I sit with the case of water on my lap and we head north.

Sure enough there's the old 85' Dodge just like he said. I thank him profusely and he's on his way. I walk down to the camp sight. On the way I find my shoe right between the road and the cypress tree where I had set up camp. My guitar is there and there's still like 3 or 4 beers. I slam them, get warm, and head to my truck with my guitar and whatever other shit I had brought down there. I sleep in the cab until dawn.

I wake up freezing my balls off, still drunk and bleary. I head back to Oakland. Probably stopped in Half Moon Bay for a little breakfast. I'm home by at least 10AM. I pull up to the church and the gate is closed and locked but the front door is wide open. I left town for 24 hours with the fucking door to my home wide oped in the fucking hood. What a genius I am. A few weeks later I realize that anyone could have reached into the gate, pulled up the steal rod that gos down into the cement and pulled the gate open to jack all of my shit. There's hoops in the apparatus for a padlock which I immediately install.

I got a pass that day quite a few times over. Did I walk south on Highway 1? Did I walk south down the beach? Who the fuck knows. My shoe was between the camp site and the highway, so maybe highway. But then why the fuck was I climbing out of the bushes and plants and shit on the side of the road when dude started shining his flashlight in my eyes. I suppose this is a mystery that will be revealed through hypnosis someday. Yeah right, hypnosis is bullshit.

-DUTCHESS & THE DUKE TOUR DIARY 2009-

Day 1: Sacramento, CA @ Luigi's Fun Garden. Saturday, November 7th, 2009.

Woke up in Oakland with a hangover. Had been up late the night before drinking whiskey with Roadhouse. Slept on his couch. Went to breakfast with him, Kris, Lizzy, Carlos, and Oscar at *The Hideaway*, which is a little restaurant by The Coast Guard Base in Alameda run by a crazy old Korean lady.

Went back to Roadhouse's place after that. Waited for Oscar to get ready to hit the road. Me and Kris laid on the couch. Glaze decided he wanted to go with us. So me, Oscar and him jumped in the car and headed for Sacramento. Met up with Jesse and Kimberly at some friend of Mitch's house. We practiced, I bought a new tambourine. Played sober that night to a quiet and attentive crowd. Met some cute girls that I did not fuck, then started to get drunk in preparation for the *D & D* set.

We played pretty good for one practice and many drinks each. It was a lot of fun. They had a creepy super fan there that had driven all the way from Idaho. By the end of the night he was inviting himself along with us and we were mercilessly bagging on him. What a bunch of pricks we are. Ended up staying with some grad-students in Davis. Took a Xanax that didn't do shit. Slept on the floor. Made fun of Kimberly's eyebrows. Her and Jesse are really cool. They got good senses of humor, thick skin, and I can't get their songs out of my head. Oscar is girl crazy and constantly whining about pussy. Hopefully someone fucks him on this trip so he'll shut the fuck up. Hung out with Black Jay too.

Day 2: San Francisco, CA @ The Bottom of the Hill. Sunday, November 8th, 2009.

Woke up with a hangover on a floor in Davis. Had coffee. Drove to East Oakland to have breakfast with everyone. The people we stayed with last night were very nice. One of the girls had an extremely powerful hug. Dually noted by myself and Glaze. *D & D* played an in-store. They were good. I felt like I was gonna die. Went to The City at six for sound check, ate, waited. Drank a bottle of wine around nine, played at ten. Drunk, but completely in control. Did pretty good I think, then *D & D*. I was dancing around the stage like a moron yelling, "Clap you fucking faggots!" Had a lot of fun. Went to Josh Miller's with Alexis.

Day 3: Oakland, CA Off. Monday, November 9th, 2009.

Woke up hungover on Josh's couch. He kicked us out when he went to work in the morning. Me and Alexis wondered the city for a couple hours. We said our goodbyes, I went back to Oakland. Showered, tried to nap. Me and Kris made dinner at her house in the evening. Fried green tomatoes, corn, greens, red beans and rice. *D & D* came over with Jason and Oscar. Didn't drink or smoke all day.

<u>Day 4: Santa Cruz, CA @ The Crepe Place. Tuesday,</u>
<u>November 10th, 2009.</u>

Woke up not hungover, but had bad insomnia. Probably slept four hours in all. Sound was shit tonight. Crowd was OK. Eran came to the show, and a bunch of people from The Bay Area. Eran was hilarious ordering his dinner. "I do not like sour cream so that would not work." Went camping afterwards, got fucked up, and sang Hank Williams songs with Kimberly. I don't think she's that attractive, got no eyebrows, but I wanna fuck her, just to fuck her. Slept in the back seat of Eran's car. Thought I would freeze to death.

<u>Day 5: Los Angeles, CA @ Spaceland. Wednesday,</u>
<u>November 11th, 2009.</u>

Woke up dirty and hungover. Took the 101 down to LA, long drive, sucked. I rode shotgun and played radio nazi. Uneventful night, scratch that, show was good. Afterwards, well I'm not really sure of the sequence of events, but we went to a bar. Me and Jesse try to hit on some trashy psychos. Got real fucked up. Then I poured a beer on Jesse's head while he was driving. Not really sure why. Just got tired of hearing him talk I guess. He pulled over and threw me out of the car. I sat on the sidewalk for a minute before he came back. I have never regretted doing something so much as this. A betrayal on my part. He took me on tour to help me, an altruistic and selfless act, and then I shit on him. I apologized but I don't think things will ever be the same. Blacked out later. I think I made out with Kimberly, not sure. We woke up in bed together. Didn't fuck, couldn't have gotten my dick hard anyways and Oscar told me I took some pills maybe.

Day 6: Long Beach, CA @ Alex's Bar. Thursday, November 12th, 2009.

Woke up hungover at someone's house. Oscar's dad picked me and him up. We went and helped him move a water heater to an apartment complex that he owns. Laid around his house all day. Met *D & D* at *Alex's Bar* in Long Beach. Place was awesome. I weaseled my way into opening the show with my instrumental stuff. Met a cute Asian girl and her sister. She might have been a lesbian, not sure. Went back to Bo's house after the show. She didn't come. We did some coke. Tried to make out with Kimberly but she wasn't having it. I showed her an idea for a new song and she liked it. Working on the lyrics now.

Day 7: Irvine, CA @ UC Irvine. Friday, November 13th, 2009.

Woke up hungover on a couch with Kimberly. Jesse went back to LA after the show last night to try and fuck some chick. He was unsuccessful, which was predictable, but too bad. Dude said he hasn't gotten laid in like a year. Sittin' around Oscar's folks house now. Got kinda drunk during the day for the first time on the trip. Probably not a good idea, we'll see.

Wasn't a good idea. Drank coffee and felt crazy all day. Got to the college and started slamming wine. I played really well and the audience was quiet and really into it. Read the *Medicine Fuck Dream* letter and sold like $65 in merch. Went back to Oscar's parents, didn't drink. Couldn't sleep. Me and Kimberly stayed up talking till late. Think I finally got to bed around 5AM.

Day 8: San Diego, CA @ The Casbah. Saturday, November 14th, 2009.

Laid around at Oscar's all day. The house is nice. His parents are really living the American dream. Immigrants that made it out of poverty. Short drive to San Diego, everybody else went to get sushi. I ate a *Subway* to save money. Been waisting way too much cash on partying and food. Also getting tired of 24/7 stupid jokes. Need a break from the banter. This show was decent. Can't remember where we stayed, probably got fucked up.

Day 9: Phoenix, AZ @ The Rhythm Room. Sunday, November 15th, 2009.

Club was some blues bar. Got royally fucked up this night. Got booed at the show. Crowd was loud and didn't give a fuck for the most part. They were good for *D & D*. Went to a bar afterward, beat both *D & D* at pool. Kimberly got pissed at me for rubbing her crotch with a pool cue. She said I kept trying to smoke in the bar. We slept in the foyer of someones parent's house on tile. Walked to the bank and payed my credit card bill the next day.

Day 10: Flagstaff, AZ off. Monday, November 16th, 2009.

Went to Flagstaff, had horrible pizza, got a cheap motel. Went to the bar at *Chile's* while Jesse masturbated in the motel room. Had a few beers, crashed at midnight.

Day 11: Albuquerque, NM @ The Launchpad. Tuesday, November 17th, 2009.

Show kinda sucked. Saw Jill and Juliet. Saw the dudes from *Lover*. Went to *Burt's Tiki Lounge* after, turned 29 at midnight. Stayed at someone's house that didn't have a shower. Instead of a cake we ate bagel bites to celebrate.

Day 12: Denver, CO @ The Larimer Lounge. Wednesday, November 18th, 2009.

Drove all fucking day with a K-pin hangover. Well I didn't drive, guess I'm not going to this whole trip. Fine by me. Phil Boyland came to the show. Was nice to catch up. Show was OK, got drunk, saw *Lover* dudes again. Stayed at Phil's, got drunk with Kimberly, stayed up way too late. Sent a bunch of nasty emails to the *Scion* people and to *Birdman* when I was drunk. Really worried about that, Fuck!

PS: Looked at the emails a few days later and none were that bad.

<u>Day 13: Salt Lake City @ Kilby Court. Thursday,</u>
<u>November 19th, 2009.</u>

This show is gonna suck. Cold as fuck here. Gotta do two shows with *D & D* tonight. The drive was nine hours. They woke me up at 8AM. We are here two hours early for no fucking reason. We did stop and eat bull testicles in Wyoming, so that was interesting. Kind of chewy. They were breaded and fried, might as well have been chicken nuggets.

Made 20 bucks at the first show, might have sold a record, can't recall. I guess it was OK, people were quiet. The next show of the evening I just played drums. Guess it went OK. Kimberly was bummed before the show, tour depression I guess. I cheered her up with some Hank Williams. Played good, stayed at some asshole's house and played *Tetris*. Also, forgot we went to a goth/punk party after the show. Shit was whack. I guess we all started talking a bunch of shit.

<u>Day 14: Jackson, WY @ some art gallery. Friday,</u>
<u>November 20th, 2009.</u>

Drive here was cold and beautiful. Show was packed except nobody gave a fuck, only thing to do in town I guess. Tried to play a Hank Williams song to entertain the crowd, but that only worked for a couple minutes. *D & D* faired better. Went to a party at the house we stayed at later. They had a keg, I blacked out. In the morning, Oscar told me I told one of the guys we were staying with his eyes were too close together and he was inbred and should never have a kid because they would be inbred cracker spawn too. Then he said I walked into the other room and passed out face first on the living room floor. Oscar said all night the guy kept threatening to kick me in the ribs, but Oscar saved me. Woke up next to Kimberly in the morning.

Day 15: Boise, ID @ some club. Saturday, November 21rst, 2009.

Oscar was pissed all morning. I had chicken fried steak for breakfast again. Ate at *Pollo Rey* for dinner cuz I didn't wanna go to the whack ass pho place with no Vietnamese people working there. This show was OK. Stayed in a short bus that night that had been converted into a bedroom. It was very nice. I guess in the night I talked a bunch of shit to Kimberly. Woke up in the morning on the bed with no blankets. Kimberly on the floor with all the blankets. She makes my blood boil and I guess I do the same to her. Gotta quit being so mean to her. She is a beautiful person.

Day 16: Portland, OR @ The Doug Fir. Sunday, November 22nd, 2009.

This show was great. They gave us lots of booze and dinner. Saw Bob, Jonna, and Shannon. I played well. Me and Bob got fucked up. They gave us rooms in the attached hotel. Me and Kimberly bunked together and let Bob stay in our room. I passed out before Collin got back with the cocaine thank God.

119

Day 17: Portland to Seattle. Monday, November 23rd, 2009.

Woke up in the morning and had to do this internet thing. Got loaded in the morning with Bob on *Tullamordew* and he decided to go to Seattle with us. Polished off the bottle on the car ride. Took care of a bunch of boring shit like returning the van, unloading equipment etc......Then went to the bar across from where Kimberly was staying. Met Trevor, Tony Ching Chang, and Brad Dunn at the bar. Went on a wild goose chase for coke with Anthony and Brad. Ended up in the burbs at Brad's. Stayed up all night and realized how much of a freak both Brad and Anthony are.

Day 18: Seattle, WA @ some coffee shop. Tuesday, November 24th, 2009.

Woke up at Brad's, what a mistake. Kimberly called me all night to come back to her place, but the cab I called never came. I walked around in the burbs for an hour or so in the morning and finally got a cab back to Kimberly's place. We had the best day. We went to *The Bodies* exhibit, a couple museums, had beers at some pinball place and fucked. It was kinda like our first date. The show that night was not with *D & D*. The audience pretty much consisted of my Seattle friends that are connected to Josh, Vik, Bob, and Trevor. Brad Dunn was supposed to play but he got too fucked up.

Day 19: Seattle, WA @ The Tractor Tavern. Wednesday, November 25th, 2009.

I am so obsessed with pussy. It's not only pussy, it's women in general. I like getting them to fuck me just as much as fucking them. Anyways, this is one of the best pieces of ass I have ever gotten. Got a fucking temper though. When I find out how to push someone's buttons I will, which is going to become a problem with her I know. I think I'm in love with her. She has a beautiful voice. Anyways, Josh and Anthony met up with me at the club early to get dinner. Kimberly and some music journalist chick drug us to some insanely expensive Italian restaurant. I wanna say it was like $60 to $80 a person. When we got the bill Josh was pissed. He's a cheap fuck, I was pissed too.

I played good that night, eventually won over the crowd. Had to play electric. Ended with "Apple Pie and Genocide" with Oscar on the bass and Donny on drums. Donny played drums for *D & D* that night. I got drunk. They were good. I did a couple songs with them, they ended the set in tears. Weird mofos. Finally got out of there and went to some shitty party. Did some coke, fell asleep.

Day 20: Seattle to Oakland, Thanksgiving. Thursday, November 26th, 2009.

Kimberly missed her flight this morning, don't remember where to. She didn't care and that meant I had a ride to the airport for my flight. Fucked again. She's a

121

nympho, I love it! Roadhouse picked me up from the airport and we went to Kris'. Dinner was great, but I was a zombie. Got Bronzo's keys so I could sleep it off in peace at his place. Just can't socialize anymore.

Day 21: Oakland, off. Friday, November 27th, 2009.

Woke up feeling great today. Went to the warehouse to make instrumental mixes of a bunch of *Mirrors* stuff for the *Scion* website. They say they'll give me $400 a song, so hopefully they take a few. Sent Adam Shore the tracks, went to Kris' in the evening and fucked her brains out.

Day 22: Oakland, off. Saturday, November 28th, 2009.

Went and got Mexican breakfast in East Oakland. Kris had stuff to do today so I went and hung out with Roadhouse. We shot the shit for a while, had a beer, and then went to the pencil dick liquor store. Coming out we ran into Damon and he invited us to a party Wallace was having that afternoon. He made a fuck ton of jambalaya. We got loaded on cheap beer, then Ben calls me. Ben is my favorite roommate at the warehouse right now. He's a junky. Kris gets to the party. The logical next step, since it's 6pm and we are all shit-canned, is to buy cocaine, but Damon cant score any. We go to *Eli's* and have a beer. Then I get a genius fucking idea. Why don't we call Ben, score some H and do it at the warehouse when we are all piss drunk and it could possibly fucking kill us. So that's what we did. We snorted heroin. Tiny lines of heroin, it was weird. I'd never done it before. It crept up slow. All of a sudden all I could do was lay in bed. Damon let me, House, and Kris have his room for the night. I don't know if I slept or not but I felt fucking wonderful. House puked and went home, then I spent hours trying to convince Kris that me, her and Lisa should have a polygamous relationship. She didn't seem to think that would work. Had to try.

Day 23: Oakland, off. Sunday, November 29th, 2009.

Recovering all day. Nothing really to tell. Kind of sucked.

Day 24: Oakland, off. Monday, November 30th, 2009.

Tying up loose ends, getting ready to fly to Chicago tomorrow. Me and Kris saw *The Road*. I thought it was boring. Stayed at Bronzo's.

Day 25: Oakland to Chicago, off. Tuesday, December 1rst, 2009.

Flew into Chicago, landed in the early evening. Kimberly met me at the airport. We kissed and held each other on the train. Met up with Billiams and went to a couple of bars. Then decided to just get some booze and go back to Billiams' place. We started on wine and then graduated to Middle Man (a drinking game). The game ended when I puked up a mixture of red wine and cheep beer on the kitchen table, I think it was *Busch*. Fun shit.

Day 26: Chicago, IL. The King Khan and BBQ Show, off.
Wednesday, December 2nd, 2009.

Got fucked up all day. Went to see *King Khan and BBQ* at night. Got more fucked up, did coke and apparently offended a large portion of the people I know in Chicago. I guess I was trying to get Mark Sultan laid by my friend Dave's new girlfriend right in front of him. I called the bartender a faggot or a shit-head and Matt Williams slapped me around a bit. Then somehow I ended up back at Jared and Mellisa's snorting Oxycontin till 6AM.

Day 27: Chicago, off. Thursday, December 3nd, 2009.

Jesse arrives in Chicago, I feel like death all day. They practice. I download Leonard Cohen *"Live At The Isle Of White"*, It's OK. He cant sing. Makes me feel better.

Day 28: Grinnel, IA @ some college. Friday, December 4th, 2009.

Felt real fucked up this day in the car. Had to pound two beers. Billiams ran out of gas on the tollway. We stopped in Rock Island so they could do some pointless internet thing. Was pissed cuz I had to get up so early. Played the college, no-one cared, got drunk. Jesse and Billiams went to some party filled with hot sluts. Billiams went to the dorms with one of them. Fucked her in the ass in a phone booth then handcuffed her to it. Go figure........

Day 29: Chicago, IL @ The Empty Bottle. Saturday, December 5th, 2009.

First Show with Jared and Mellisa. This show sold out and I only got $150. Shiesty motherfuckers. Anyways, got drunk, had to play electric. Think I did pretty well. Saw Alex White. She's cute, met her brother, he's not. *D & D* had a violin player on this one. Stayed at the bar till late, did coke, made my apologies to everyone for the other night, and stayed at Jared and Mellisa's.

Day 30: Minneapolis, MN @ The Seventh Street Entry. Sunday, December 6th, 2009.

NO ENTRY

Day 31: Omaha, NB @ ?????????. Monday, December 7th, 2009.

We drove through a fucking blizzard today. It took ten hours to do a three hour drive. Show was decent.

Day 32: Lawrence, KS @ ?????????. Tuesday, December 8th, 2009.

Got drunk on wine tonight as always. Show was whatever, it's Kansas. Stayed with these brothers that worked at a *Walmart* distribution center. They lived a half hour out of town. It was snowing. One brother rode in the van with Billiams, Jared, Mellisa, and Kimberly. Me and Jesse road with the other brother in his car. I passed out or blacked out sometime before we left for their place. I woke up in the back of the car in a snow bank on a country road. I got out of the car and no-one was around. Jesse and homeboy left me in the back of the car to freeze to death while they got help or whatever. I walk down the country road in the snow alone for a bit and then the van pulls up. I hop in and Jesse and dude are with the rest of the band. I keep asking why the fuck they live in this shit. "You have options!" I say.

Day 33: Columbia, MO @ ?????????. Wednesday, December 9th, 2009.

    NO ENTRY

Day 34: Little Rock, AR, @ The Chicken Shack. Thursday, December 10th, 2009.

    NO ENTRY

Day 35: Denton, TX @ Rubber Gloves. Friday, December 11th, 2009.

    I played very drunk and then passed out backstage. At the end of the night the promoter asked Jesse, "Where's Greg Ashley?" Jesse pointed to the floor apparently, and there I was.

Day 36: Austin, TX @ Club Deluxe. Saturday, December 12th, 2009.

Saw Shana at this show. She looked liked Tony Soprano's wife.

Day 37: Houston, TX @ Walter's. Sunday, December 13th, 2009.

We went down to my parent's in League City before the show. I was hungover of course. Me and Kimberly played *Joker* with my mom. The neighbor girls came over and they were high as shit. It was kind of entertaining to see my mom interact with stoned teenagers now that I'm not the one. Show was OK. We got drunk and stayed at Paola's place. Did coke.

Day 38: New Orleans, LA @ Circle Bar. Monday, December 14th, 2009.

NO ENTRY

Day 39: Birmingham, AL @ ?????????. Tuesday, December 15th, 2009.

NO ENTRY

Day 40: Atlanta, GA @ ?????????. Wednesday, December 16th, 2009.

NO ENTRY

Day 41: Indianapolis, IN @ ?????????. Thursday, December 17th, 2009.

NO ENTRY

Day 42: Lafayette, IN @ Black Sparrow. Friday, December 18th, 2009.

NO ENTRY

Day 43: Milwaukee, WI @ ?????????. Saturday, December 19th, 2009.

Fairly short drive from Lafayette to Milwaukee today, which was nice. Kimberly was pissed at me all day. Not really sure what I did last night, but that's becoming a pretty common theme. We stop in Chicago to pick up Mellisa, who was supposed to do Mill with us, but Jared freaked out and wouldn't let her come after we drove to their house. Drank a lot of wine at the club. I played at 11:30 central time which was 12:30 eastern time where I came from, so I was super retarded. And this show was the last of the tour. Think I played alright. Closed the set for the first time with "True Love Leaves No Traces". Dedicated it to Kimberly, I meant it and I thought it might get me out of the doghouse. After I played I was practically blacked out and these two girls talked me into going to the beach. They fed me two Aderol. I regained self awareness at some strange hour at some strange house. Made them take me back to the bar and right when we arrived the van was pulling away and my phone was dead so I couldn't call. Tried to follow them, but that was a bust. Went to some house, made out with the blond one. Didn't want to, but she was pretty. I really wanted to be with Kimberly. It was our last night together and I squandered it. In the morning I woke to an empty house. Walked down to the bar at the end of the street. Luckily I had written down Billiam's number. Called him. Called Lisa who told me she wasn't coming to Chicago cuz she had to take care of her dog Toki, she had a new boyfriend and the road conditions were terrible. I cried and drank all day. I was devastated.

-BOYS TOWN-

Me and Roadhouse used to go down to Nuevo Laredo sometimes when we were 18 or 19. I think he went at least once with Chad after I moved. First time we went down there was in the old red pickup my dad gave me. I guess it wasn't that old back then. I still drive it. It's not exactly what it used to be. Anyways, I can't remember what time of year it was cuz it's always hot in South Texas. I remember straightening my legs while I was driving so the air from the vent would go up my pants to cool my balls. The AC was busted, still is.

We drive across the border and get a motel. Some dump, I can't remember the name. We walk down the street and start hitting the bars, getting fucked up. Some other white motherfucker brought a bottle of whiskey into the bar we were hangin' at and started pouring everybody shots. The bartender didn't give a fuck. People kept telling us, "You gotta go to *Boy's Town*, you gotta go to *Boy's Town*." They tell us, "Just get in any cab and tell them to take you to *Boy's Town*. It'll be like ten bucks."

So we hail a cab. Cab drives us around town and slightly out of the city. We come up to a wall, a tall one made of concrete. We drive around this structure and through some iron gates. And what are we let out into? That scene in *From Dusk Till Dawn*, the Tarantino film where Cheech Marin is talking about all the different kinds of pussy. "Alright, pussy pussy pussy, come on in pussy lovers. We got white pussy, black pussy, Spanish pussy, yellow pussy. We got hot pussy, cold pussy, wet pussy, smelly pussy. We got silk pussy, velvet pussy, snapping

pussy, we even got horse pussy, dog pussy," etc.......
There's a dude doing a similar spiel outside of this club.
There's a whole city of whore houses, bars and strip clubs
inside these walls. We are told it used to be a women's
prison.

We start wandering. Mainly we're actually just looking
for a regular shit-hole bar, which we eventually find, but
first we are ushered into many strip clubs and bars that do
this. They sit you down, you order a drink. Two prostitutes
come and sit at your table, order a drink on your tab, and
start trying to fuck you. Guess I never found the right girl.
We try to steer clear of these places once we figure out
what they look like, and how much some asshole out front
is trying to get you to come in and watch the donkey show
or some other bullshit like that.

I remember one, they had the donkey out front and I
checked it out. It was a female donkey, but they were
advertising that the donkey was gonna fuck some chick or
she was gonna suck it's dick or something.

Anyways, you go into one of these joints and two
things always happen: Number one, two she-males come
and sit on your lap at your table and start ordering drinks
on your tab. The other thing is, the donkey never does any
fucking. So no donkey show. Finally we find a somewhat
normal joint. The bar in this place has a trough under the
stools so you can just piss right there. Don't have to leave
the bar ever. We drink, we play pool, then we stumble into
The Western, a she-male bar, fuck that. We see the two old
guys that have the room next to us in the motel we rented.
They strut right into *The Western* with their cowboy hats
on. Cool.

We go to some other bars where motherfuckers don't bother you. There was one I really liked. I wonder if it's still there. It had leather chairs and wood paneling, very comfortable. Eventually we get a cab back to the motel, crash, and drive back to League City in the morning.

On the way back, on highway 59, we get stopped at a checkpoint and the pigs search the truck. I was using a guitar case as my suitcase and they thought that was weird. Also we were coming back from Mexico so they were sure we had drugs. They separate us. We're sitting on the side of the highway in the desert, it's 100 degrees plus out in the sun, and they take apart my tailgate. The cops come over to me, "Your friend told us where all the drugs are hidden in the truck. You might as well come clean." Well this is news to me, do tell. Finally they let us go. Fuck Texas cops. Worst motherfuckers on the planet. I used to hate all cops, then I moved to Oakland and realized not all cops are assholes. That is, as long as you're white.

Another time we went down to Nuevo Laredo with a whole crew. It was Trey, Chad, Sam, Roadhouse, Rob, and me. We get a motel. While there, Chad kicks in the door to the bathroom and takes a picture of House taking a dump. We use it for a *Mirrors* flyer later. I also get the flyer blown up to ten times its original size and hang it on the wall of my apartment. People sometimes ask Roadhouse when they meet him. "You look really familiar. I've seen you somewhere."

"Greg's wall," he tells them.

We go to the pharmacia to buy pills. Rob buys Phenol Barbital, which none of us knew at the time is just a hardcore sleeping pill that killed a bunch of famous people back in the 1960's when they mixed it with booze. We all take a pill and sleep for like four hours. Waste of time and money that was, fucking Rob. I love the guy but Jesus.

Then we're off to *Boy's Town*. Same shit, donkey show, she-males, trough. We fall into all the same traps, then finally end up at the trough bar. We get fucked up there for a while then hit the dusty streets again. Chad and Trey go into some room with a hooker and take pictures of her naked and shit. Not a good lookin' broad. She steals Trey's wallet or he loses it. He tells the federales, they arrest her, then he get's them to let her go. She punches him and insults him in Spanish, good for her. Fuck the police.

We accidentally stumble into *The Western*. Me and Roadhouse are last in line to enter. Hookers just come out of the woodwork instantly, start grabbing at all of us. Roadhouse is right behind me, and right away grabs my ass and pulls me back out the door. "That's the she-male bar from last time with the old guys."

"Oh shit you're right," I say. We walk across the street and sit on the sidewalk against a wall. I have a bottle of tequila we start working on.

Slowly, one by one, all of our friends start filtering out of *The Western*. Chad says, "Man there's something weird going on in there."

Trey comes out, "What the fuck? Why'd you guys bail on me? Sam and Rob are sitting at a table with a bunch of she-males. They ordered a bunch of drinks."

"No shit," says Roadhouse. We sit there on the corner drinking tequila.

Sam comes out. "What the fuck, that was terrible. And

Rob just went in the back with a she-male."

Rob comes out of the building doing his finger snap, slap hand move that many of us picked up after a while. I still do it sometimes. What Bob used to call, "Another dirty little habit picked up from Rob." That's rich.

Rob, "I just got my dick sucked."

Chad, "You know those were all dudes right?"

"Na man, what the fuck? Na, I had my fingers in some muff man. I felt that shit."

Either Rob didn't give a fuck, or he was into it, but I will say this. Rob did comment on a couple of occasions that evening about how believable some of the lady boys were. Good times. We all head back to League City with hangovers.

-GRIS GRIS ON THE CANADIAN BORDER-

It was Saturday April 8th, 2006. Twelve years ago today as this is being written. I know the date cuz I found an old email. We were headed for Toronto, which was always one of the best cities for us on tour. We were coming from Kalamazoo, MI. I woke up very hungover this day. I think we all did. We had all gone to some party the night before after our show. I don't remember it at all because I blacked out before we got there and immediately passed out in a chair at the party according to Lars.

Anyways, we pull up to the border between Detroit and Windsor Ontario, everything is in order except for our merch. Our documents are printed and we have everything set up to purchase our work visa that costs roughly $400. I tell Oscar to take off his sunglasses, which he doesn't. I know the border patrol wants to see the whites of your eyes when you pull up to their window. And they'd probably really wanna see Oscar's since he's Mexican and has a beard like Fidel Castro. The FOBs at his work call him "El Taliban". Mind you that this is when people still gave a shit about the wars in Iraq and Afghanistan. This was the Bush era. Everyone was paranoid about some overblown terrorist threat from the middle east. Me, Oscar, Joe, and Glaze are in the rental car. Lars "The Siberian Tickler" and Roadhouse are in my mom's old minivan behind us with all the gear. I pull up to the window and hand the agent all of our passports and driver's licenses. The agent peers into the rental and doesn't seem to like what he sees. I tell him the minivan behind us is with us too. He takes our identification and documents and looks them over for a minute. He goes on his computer and does whatever for a while.

"OK everything is in order here, but all of your IDs are completely covered in cocaine." We didn't know this, but at the Canadian border the agents have some sort of scanner they can put your driver's license in that detects cocaine residue. He directs us to pull into some area where they can search the car. We pull over, they bring out the drug dog. The dog smells something in the car. The van pulls into another stall. They don't search it or talk to Lars or Roadhouse.

They ask me how much merchandise we have. I estimate. They tear apart the car looking for non-existent drugs. They take the four of us that were in the rental into a building and strip search us one by one. Some old British cunt is in charge. He says to me, "I'm not going to touch you and you're not going to touch me." OK, I think, not so bad. He has me take off my clothes one piece at a time. "OK, bend over and spread your cheeks. Alright, lift up your boys." And I'm done.

Whatever, they're the ones that will have to suffer. I'm the only one that had a shower that day, let alone that week. Joe is traumatized by all this. He has never done cocaine, he is pissed. Some of the powder must have rubbed off on his ID from the rest of ours.

When they're done looking in our assholes they count every piece of merchandise. Then they compare it to the estimate I gave them. When all is said and done I had underestimated. "This is what we have tallied and this is what you have. You can pay the taxes on everything that you claimed and the rest you can either pay a fine or we can destroy for you." How nice of him to offer. We pay the fine. It was $900 for the merch taxes and fines plus the $400 for our work visa.

All this took hours. The clock is ticking and we are running out of time to get to Toronto. Then they find mace in Oscar's bag. Someone had given it to him for some reason along the road. Boarder guard tells us, "Mace is illegal in Canada, it would usually be a $300 fine, but I am going to help you lads out. Mr. Ashley and Mr. Michel, you need to take the mace and this document across the bridge back to Detroit. Give them to the American authorities and they will dispose of the mace. Bring the document back signed and you are free to go." Great, I think, at this point I would rather just pay the 300 bucks than drive back and forth across this border again.

So it's back to Detroit. I give the border cops the letter. "OK, pull over and go into that building." We pull over. Right then a Detroit cop yells, "We got a runner!" Ten Detroit pigs stampede out of the building, guns drawn. It ends up being a false alarm. They all look a bit dejected. We enter the building and I hand over the document and the mace. We sit there for ten minutes or so, then are told, "Get outa' here."

So we're out the door, headed back to the car, when we see an American agent snooping around our vehicle. Oscar has left his digital camera in there and this cop is looking through the pictures. Cop looks up, "Go back inside right now."

My mind scrolls back through the expanse of drunken time to a few nights earlier at Gene's house in Columbus, OH. We always stayed with Gene. He had a gigantic house, was a nice guy, and always had a shit load of cocaine. Plenty to share, which he always did. Everybody stayed with Gene. One time I woke up at his place and Cyrus from *Drunk Horse* was in his kitchen hitting the bong. "Grashley!"

I'm confused, "What the hell are you doing here?"

Cyrus, "Hangin' with Gene."

It's then I remember, Roadhouse had taken pictures of all of us snorting coke at Gene's house and this fucking pig was getting an eyeful of incriminating evidence.

So now we're back in the building. They take me into the interrogation room first. There's two cops. Big middle eastern dude and a white motherfucker. White cop lifts me up by my shirt. "You're gonna tell me where all the fucking drugs are that are hidden in that car. If you don't and we find something, you and your friend are going to jail."

Me, "Look, I know what you must have seen on the camera, but you gotta believe me, there are no drugs hidden in that car. We're just a band trying to get to our gig in Toronto."

White cop, "Should we believe him?"

Middle eastern cop, "No."

They pull out a box of tinctures that some hippie chick gave us in Atlanta. We played at her tea house earlier in the tour. She said the tinctures would "cleanse our bodies and mind" or some bullshit. White cop asks me, "What are these? Looks like heroin."

I'm thinkin', "That's a lot of heroin that bitch gave us for free, and who rolls around with viles of liquid heroin?" He tests it. Surprise! It's not fucking heroin dip-shit.

They send me out and pull Oscar in. I wait. I can hear them yelling at him. Then all of a sudden Oscar bolts out of the room. "Let's go, get up."

I look up at Oscar, "Uh, OK."

White cop yells, "Yeah, get the fuck out of here you idiots! You're lucky we don't send the Canadians those pictures!"

We head back across The Ambassador Bridge. This little errand has taken over an hour. We get back to the other side where everybody else has been waiting for us with the Canadian Border Patrol. Joe asks me, "What took you guys so long?"

"There was a line. Let's go, we're running late." I hand the signed paper to the Canadians. We drive.

We stop for our second meal of Taco Bell that day and me and Oscar relay the story of what just happened to the rest of the guys. We make it to Toronto just in time for our set. We play well and make a bunch of money. Enough, I guess, to offset the $1300 and seven hours of horse shit we just went through. The venue we played at lost it's liquor license a couple hours before we got there, so we can't even drink away our pain. The next morning Lars finds the mace in his bag. Either the American authorities were confused, or they planted it back on us. Who knows. We threw the mace in the trash and went on with our lives.

-BRONZO & THE BROKEN TAP-

Jay Bronzini was one of the sweetest guys you could know. He always looked out for his pals. He was certainly a scrappy motherfucker. There was some bar fight at a *Time Flys* Show back in the day and Jay just stepped in and started fucking dudes up. Wasn't his fight at all. Either Eric or Andy, did or said something fucked up, and shit ensued.

Playing in a band with him was a lot of fun. He was a great drummer and we both liked to party and just generally didn't give a fuck. Between me and Jay and Eric's antics (Josh was the reasonable and somewhat well behaved one of the quartet) we got banned from quite a few clubs in San Francisco. We could give two shits, plus people that run venues seem to have pretty short memories. Well, except for *The Rickshaw Stop* in San Francisco, they never seem to forget. I haven't played there in like eight or nine years. Old Dan Stracota, that books that place, seems to have the memory of an elephant.

SLVR got banned from there because we were late for a show we were supposed to be opening. We didn't think that the club would actually want us to go on at 8pm or whatever it was. Eric was in a lamaze class with his wife Jenny till late that day. All of us except for him got to the club early. We couldn't get a hold of him, he had no cell phone. Eric finally shows up and we get to play three songs before the sound guy tells us we are done. I tell him we are not and continue to play. Eventually he cuts the mics, so I verbally abuse his tight ass. We are 86ed.

Now I'm not personally banned from there yet, not

yet........ For years I could pretty much count on doing a solo gig there around once a month. The booker liked what I did, so he'd throw me on the opening slot for whatever indie garbage was coming through each month. It was always a $100 guarantee, which was great, it was pretty much the only paycheck I could count on. Then I fucked that up. Dan gave me a gig opening for some Irish folk duo, pretty gay shit but who cares, it's money.

I had just recorded my instrumental album, and I was itching to play that material live with a band. I hadn't played with a band in years and I had one all ready to go from recording. Everybody said they could do the show, so we did. I didn't bother telling the club what I had planned because I'm an inconsiderate prick. I figured we were playing first and wouldn't need to bother with the PA since it was going to be all instrumental anyways. I get there with all the guys and the sound guy kind of freaks out. I tell him to calm down and just hang out, "Look, you don't have to mic any of this stuff. The drums are plenty loud and we have amps for everything." The sound guy insists on doing his job, whatever. We play and people like it.

A bunch of friends come to the show, Roadhouse, Kris, Matt, Wallace, Tony etc..... Matt's on bass and Wallace is on sax. Little Tony is on the drums. We're all hanging out backstage partying, then Matt comes in and starts complaining about how the bouncer forced his way into the bathroom when he was taking a shit. I didn't really think much about it at the time. We all continue to drink the night away.

Once the show is over, I go to find whoever the manager was that evening to get paid. "You know your bass player was shooting up in the bathroom, and one of your friends drank the headliners bottle of wine."

I say, "Man, that didn't happen. Come on. There's gotta be some kind of misunderstanding or something. They didn't do those things."

"Oh yes they did, they did."

I'm unsure at this point, but I figure if I'm going with confidant denial already, I might as well stick with this tactic. "Well I gotta get going, so I was wondering if I could get paid?"

"Here." He hands me an envelope with $100 dollars in it. I never heard from them again, and actually don't think I've set foot in that place since that night. I don't generally travel across the bay to see crap in an over-sized dance hall that is nowhere near any BART stations.

I get into the van after all the gear is loaded. "Roadhouse, did you drink the headliner's wine?"

"Well yeah, they left it back there when they went on stage. Why not? They weren't drinking it." I don't even bother to ask Matt any questions. We go back to Oakland.

SLVR was also banned from *Slims*. We were late again. This time it was my fault. I was sleeping off a cocaine bender while we were supposed to be sound checking. Josh is at the club in San Francisco patiently waiting for the rest of us (he lives over there) while Eric and Jay are trying to get into *The Ghost-town* to wake me up. They've been calling me for hours. Finally they get let in. They go around back, climb in my window, and pull me out of bed. We get to the venue just in time to play our set. I asked Josh about this incident the other day. He tells me we played poorly, but that for once I was the most sober out of the bunch since I had been sleeping all day, instead of drinking all day, like Jay and Eric.

After our set we sit backstage and, what else? We drink. The staff is continually giving us shit for smoking inside. We ignore them. Eventually Jay tears down the non-smoking sign in our room because hey, no sign, no rule. Josh tells me when he goes to get paid the booker gives him this kind of sympathetic look and says, "You know you can never play here again right?"

Josh looks back at him and says, "Yeah, yeah I know." Of course we did a few years later.

We pissed off venues up and down the coast. We didn't play out of town really ever, so I guess when we did, it was just in our nature to make a night of it. You know, being a special occasion and all. Eric was married with a kid, so when he got to go out, he went for it. Me and Jay were just dirt-bags and Josh was along for the ride.

We played down in Monterey once. That was strange. At one point we're standing outside the club we're playing at, having a smoke, and the cops pull up. They come up the wrong way on a one-way street, jump out of their squad car and apprehend Josh. The pigs run his license and then release him. They say they're looking for a suspect that fits his description (long hair with a leather jacket) but it's not him, so he can go back to smoking. Thanks Mr. Piggy. Jesus, I wonder what happens to black people when they try to hang out in Monterey? Just a warning to my brothers in Oakland, if they're fucking with white dudes in leather jackets down there, might be a place to steer clear of, being that they are operating on such vague descriptions of suspects and all.

I piss off the sound guy that night because I wont turn my amp down, but we play good and get paid and all that. Kind of a boring show. We get a motel room next to a bar. We get hammered. None of us had dinner, so we try to order a pizza but are all too fucked up to complete this simple task. Jay ends up ripping the phone out of the wall and throwing it across the parking lot. We go back to the bar to find cocaine. We meet an old veteran, around 60 or something. He's got coke. He comes back to our room and we snort some of his shitty blow. I pass out on the floor between the bed and the wall, Eric stays up all night talking to the old man, and I don't know what Josh and Jay did. I guess just passed out too. I think that weak ass blow was just no competition for all the shots we had taken.

Then there was the night Jay got a DUI coming back from a gig we did at *The Hemlock*. I met up with him earlier in the evening to load all the gear into his truck. He was already drunk. He'd been at some rich person's party on a boat all day or something. I told him I could drive. I was hungover as shit that day, and for once in my life had no real compulsion to drink. Jay tells me he's fine, that I can drive his truck home after the gig. I jump in the truck with him and we head to San Francisco.

We play, whatever, I have my two free drinks, then we load up the truck and head back to Oakland. I offer to drive. I tell Jay, "Alright give me the keys."

Jay get's into the driver's seat, "No man, I'm fine. I can drive."

"OK, if you're alright go for it, but I barely had anything to drink in there."

"Yeah, I'm fine," says Jay. I jump into the passenger

seat and we hit the road. On The Bay Bridge Jay's phone starts to ring. I tell him not to answer it, that it's illegal to talk on the phone while driving. Jay starts digging around in his pocket trying to find his cellphone, this causes him to swerve a bit.

The highway patrol pulls us over on the bridge. They come up to the window and ask the same bullshit questions as always, "Where are you guys coming from tonight? How much have you had to drink?"

Jay tells them, "Two drinks. I was swerving because I was trying to find my phone to turn it off. I know you're not supposed to talk on the phone while driving, and someone was calling me."

"Sir, can you step out of the car for me please?" The cops give Jay all the tests and then come back to my window. "Well your friend is going to jail, I guess you better find yourself a ride home."

"Well I can drive, I only had one drink tonight." It's a rule when talking to the police to make all your truths half truths, that's just how it is OK.

He breathalyzes me, I pass. "Why the hell weren't you driving? You know you put your life, and everyone else's life in danger tonight that was on this highway?"

"Hey, I offered, he said he was fine." Cop gets Jay's keys from him and gives them to me. I go and unload all the gear at Jays house and then pass out. I was exhausted.

Jay quit the band soon after that, but of course we still remained close friends. He played drums for me on and off for a year or two. Played on my Cohen album and found me my tape machine on *Craigslist*. He knew I needed an upgrade. He recorded bands too. He said hella a bunch, but for some reason it didn't annoy me when he did it. We continue to get into trouble together, as good friends should. Me, him, and Roadhouse sure did party it up.

Over the years, Eric and Jenny would have me house sit for them when they left town. Not because they need it, but because they know I do. Any break from the warehouse in a peaceful environment is good for my soul, and they are good friends.

The night I am going to tell you about was just like every other night had been for a long time. Getting fucked up with Bronzo and Roadhouse again. It was 2010 and the economy had crashed a couple years prior to this. Neither of them had jobs and I barely worked. If I did it was from 1 to 7pm, and my day consisted of drinking beer and hitting record. Then buying cocaine with the money I made, and continuing on with Roadhouse and Jay.

The three of us are at Eric and Jenny's. We decide to walk down to *The Avenue* for a drink. We start giving the bartender coke. He starts giving us free drinks. We are surrounded by cholos and wiggers. It's north Oakland, go figure. We're shooting whiskey and doing bumps in the bathroom for an hour or so. At one point, the bartender is away from his post for an inordinately long period of time. He might have been in the crapper doing our coke for all I can remember, but what I certainly do remember is Jay deciding that he would pour himself a *PBR*. (Why you would drink that shit when the world is your oyster I have no idea. I would have poured myself a *Coors Light* if I was him, but anyways.)

Jay reaches across the bar and plops his pint glass down under the spigot to fill his glass. Then he slips on something as he's leaning across the bar. He tries to catch himself with the tap. Bad idea. Thing broke off right in his hand, and he spilled his beer. Then all of a sudden all the wiggers and cholos in the bar lose their shit, "Ah Shit! You be fuckin' with our bar. You gonna have to pay for that boyeee." The bartender comes back. He doesn't seem to give a shit at this point from all I can tell. The wiggers continue, "Yo, what the fuck? Why you be breakin' my boy's shit?"

Me, "Alright he's sorry, I have some cash on me. How much do we owe you for the tap?"

Bartender, "It's $300."

Me, "What? that's bullshit, I'll give you fifty bucks."

Bartender, "That's how much it is. $300"

Jay rushes the door. The cholos grab him. The wiggers start punching him in the face. Jay is pinned.

Me, "What the fuck? What the fuck? Stop, fucking stop it!"

Cholo, "Call the police." Jay breaks free and hits one of the wiggers on the chin. All those fuckers jump on his ass.

Me, "Alright, calm down, fucking calm down. Stop hitting him." I turn to the bartender, "You really wanna call the cops with us doing all that cocaine with you in here?"

Bartender, "You better get rid of that shit." Bartender calls the police. I flush what's left of the drugs down the toilet. I don't remember it being enough for me to care.

The cops show up pretty quick actually, an anomaly for Oakland. Everyone in the bar talks to them all at once, spewing out their own ridiculous personal accounts of the events that just transpired. The three of us don't say shit.

147

The cops take us outside, put Jay in the back of the squad car, and tell me and Jeremy to get the hell out of there before those people come after us.

Man, we were just minding our own business, trying to have a good time. An accident happened, shouldn't have to be a big deal. Except fucking stupid people thrive on confrontation and violence.

We walk back to Eric and Jenny's and right as we are stepping onto the front porch the cops pull up and drop Jay off. Jay said they wrote him a ticket and then told him they just wanted to get him out of there before the situation escalated. Fucking Oakland cops. They're the best, as long as you're white.

So Jay liked to drink, but he couldn't smoke pot at all. He could smoke some crack though, just like me. I shouldn't have told him where the crack store was. I feel a bit responsible for his death. We were getting high one night and I didn't have a crack pipe, so we smoked the crack out of my weed pipe. Jay got super high, not on crack, on weed. That was the last time I saw him.

Jay killed himself in December of 2011. I never was told how he did it. His roommate Muz found him. Jay left a note. Some of it was to me, but I never read it. His sister has it, but she doesn't want to lend it to anybody, or type it out for obvious reasons. The only way I can read it is to drive out to the east-east bay to her house, and I don't really feel like doing that, it's too awkward.

What really killed Jay is America's shitty health care system, especially when it comes to mental illness. This was pre Obama Care when he died, though I don't know if there has been that much of an improvement.

Every summer Jay would have to go back to the loony bin for a day or two while the doctors re-calibrated his meds. He'd be released, and be as close to fine as he was ever gonna be, a least for a while. He did this pretty much on an annual basis.

Last time he went, he had lost his insurance and they told him, "Well, no insurance? Your visit will be $2,000 a day." Jay got back on the BART train, headed home, and just started drinking. That was the only way he had to cope with his mental illness.

His funeral ceremony was held at *The Chapel of the Chimes* in Piedmont. There was over a hundred people there. The place was packed to the gills, standing room only. Jenny gave a beautiful eulogy. She is really an amazing person. I'm getting choked up just thinking about it right now and it's been over seven years.

Later that month Jay was cremated and laid to rest in the San Francisco Bay. Jay's family and a group of his closest friends met up at The Berkeley Marina. We were each given a little cloth sack full of his bones and ashes. Claire brought a bottle of *Jameson*, his favorite whiskey. We toasted old Bronzo, then threw his bones in the bay with the seaweed. I hope the same is done for me when the end comes, just not in fucking Berkeley.......

-A JOHN BROTHERS WEDDING-

We were being flown to New York to play the wedding
of a couple that were patrons of *The Boot and Shoe
Service* in Oakland. A restaurant where we used to have a
weekly gig. The arrangement with the restaurant was,
$150 for two hours of music and carte blanche at the bar,
plus all the food we desired for free. That's $150 split five
ways mind you. Needless to say we got shit-canned every
Sunday night for two years on top shelf liquor while eating
extremely salty and greasy gourmet Italian cuisine. The
money we made every Sunday evening was nine times out
of ten spent on cocaine and/or more booze at *The Alley*, a
bar, across the street that had karaoke on Sunday nights. I
think at some point every one of us had gotten 86ed from
there for being too drunk and doing some fucked up shit.
They always forgot about it by next Sunday so we kept
coming back. Those were good times from what I can
remember.

So we fly to New York City where we rent a van. We
are going to do a couple gigs on the east coast before the
wedding. The first one is in NYC. It's in the basement of a
bar. The show goes fine, nothing really to write home
about. The second is in Hartford, Connecticut. Hartford is
a strange place. There's a palpable anger on the streets
there. Between black and white, rich and poor, and
douche bags and non-douche bags. People in New
England are generally fucking assholes, but this was worse
than I had ever experienced, even in Boston. I suppose I
was on one for this trip. I left my suit jacket at the bar we
played at. I blacked out and told some dude at the bar, who

150

was annoying me, that it was, "Time for me to dance on outa' here vato." I'm assuming we stayed at a motel that night.

The next day, it's over to Upstate New York, to the palatial estate of the family of the bride. We arrive at noon for absolutely no good reason except that's when they wanted us there. Turned out to be a blessing in disguise because they hadn't rented a drum set for us. Poor Jimi spent hours on the phone getting that all sorted out. They end up renting one from *Guitar Center*. For the plane tickets and what they were paying us, we really couldn't complain about getting there ten hours before we were scheduled to play.

Now these are the situations where I run into trouble. You put me in a place with nothing to do for ten hours with an ample supply of alcohol, and I'll usually end up pretty loaded by show-time.

The first four hours I sit by the fire and read my book on Shackleton's doomed expedition to The Antarctic. I left the book there accidentally, but I guess I pretty much know how it ends. Around 4pm the father of the bride comes up to me to inform me that there's beers in the garage. He was a real character. Kinda looked like Burnie from the movie *Weekend At Burnie's*. He had greeted us when we pulled up to the estate. We thought he was the grounds keeper or something. We asked for directions to the house and he gave us a story about using a toilet after Henry Kissinger had taken a shit in it. Later we all realized who he was. Nice guy. He lent me a coat.

So I go to the garage and grab a beer. The first guests to arrive are aunt, uncle and cousin of the bride. These three had come up from Houston for the nuptials. I don't know if the blood relation was from the aunt or uncle but I'm assuming it was the aunt. She had a thick New York accent. A carpet bagger. The son certainly was not. He was a Texan through and through. He had an accent that kind of reminded me of my friend "Justin Like The Boots" in Fort Worth. He was walking around like he owned the place. Drinking beer in the afternoon, joking around, fucking with people, saying to his dad, "Come on pops, lets blow this joint."

The day wears on. This family had a mansion on an estate with a black butler in a tuxedo. I thought I overheard them calling the butler Jefferson or something very stereotypical, but I think I mis-heard in the end. Eventually more guests arrive. The party lurches forward. People start to get drunk, as they do at weddings. I wonder around, drink, and eventually trade the beer for liquor. I see all the other John Brothers sitting at a table, laughing and joking with the aunt. Seems like things are gettin' pretty loose. I take a seat with the others. They're not exactly having an appropriate conversation with this lady, and she's fucking loaded, so I'm thinkin' great! We're all just fucking around. I try to strike up a conversation. "So, you're from Houston? That's where I grew up."

Aunt says, "Yeah."

So I say, "Well that's funny, cuz you don't sound like you're from Texas motherfucker."

"What the fuck did you just say to me?!"

"What? Nothing, just your accent-"

"What the fuck! Mark! Mark! Where's my husband? Mark!"

Oh shit. Some unholy missed communication has just occurred and I need to get the fuck out of here. I'm assuming that the big ugly fucker that was with aunt and cousin is her husband Mark, and this crazy bitch is gonna tell him some crazy shit. I go hide out by the rental and smoke a couple cigarettes. I probably stayed out there for about twenty minutes or so, just trying to let things calm down a little. What I don't know is that while I'm hiding, events are transpiring inside that are in no way helping my current situation.

Mark walks up to the table that Thatcher, Jimi, and Arlo are sitting at. "Where's the other guy?"

Thatcher, "Other guy?"

Mark, "Where's the son of a bitch that called my wife a motherfucker?"

Jimi, "Listen I think that everybody has had a little to drink and-"

Mark staring down at Thatcher, "I want you to tell me exactly what he said. Exactly."

Thatcher, "You-don't-sound-like-you're-from-Texas......motherfucker, sounds like you're from New York."

As this is happening I'm walking back up from the Suburban we rented. I slip through the crowd looking out for Mark. I'm trying to find the other guys to get a read on what it was that was perceived I said, or did, so I can either avoid or diffuse this whole situation. Then it happens, a hand on my shoulder. A big hand. I turn. It's Mark, "What in the hell did you say to my wife?"

Me, "Look I think there was a misunderstanding and-"

Mark, "Did you call my wife a motherfucker?"

Now it really wouldn't make much sense for me to call this guy's wife a motherfucker. He's obviously the motherfucker here. Even though yes, technically, I did call his wife a motherfucker. I guess you could say that. But I really only did if you take motherfucker out of context. I was using it as a term of endearment.

Me, "No, of course not. You see, we were all sitting around joking and-"

Mark, "Oh really! Cuz that's not what they said." Mark points to the table where my supposed comrades are seated. Thatcher turns his head away and looks down at the floor. They all do! They've sold me out. Traitors. Those motherfuckers.

"Look I don't know what your wife thinks she heard but-"

"You're going to apologize to my wife. Right now!"

"Like I said, I think there's been a big misunderstanding here."

Mark again, "Are you calling my wife a liar?"

"Of course not, I-"

"You're going to apologize to my wife."

Now this is the point where I start to get a bit agitated. This fat fuck. This rich, entitled piece of shit. He's probably been pushing people around his whole life. Especially if he's really from Houston. Fucking bully. Well two can play at this game. Things escalate. "I'm not apologizing to anyone. I didn't do anything wrong."

"You're going to apologize to my wife. I spent $40,000 on this wedding. You think at a classy wedding like this, it's appropriate to call a woman a motherfucker?"

I suppose this wedding was classy, maybe. I'd seen my

fair share playing with these guys. Mark's wife though? Classy? Gimmie a fuckin' break. Bitch is wearing a cheetah fur coat and she's wasted at 5pm. I mean, so am I, wasted, but I don't go around calling myself classy or anything.

"I'm not apologizing to your wife."

"Well then you're going to have to leave."

"OK. I don't give a fuck. Guys, you can have my cut of the pay. Fuck this, I'm leaving."

"Good," Mark says.

I walk out the door and head back to the rental to smoke. Arlo walks up. I tell him, "I'm not playing this gig. Fuck that guy and fuck his wife. I'm not apologizing. Fuck this."

"Come on, just apologize and this will all be over."

"Fuck that! I didn't do a goddamn thing."

The cousin walks up with Jimi and Thatcher. "Come on man, it's my little cousin's wedding, the whole family is here, the show must go on and all that, you know?"

Jimi, "Yeah Greg, just go in there and say you're sorry even if you didn't-"

Me, "Yeah, I didn't do shit! That's the whole fucking point!"

Cousin, "Well what does she think you said?"

Jimi, "He said, you don't sound like you're from Texas motherfucker."

Cousin, "Ah man, that's all. Man, I call my mom a motherfucker all the time. Let me go talk to my folks. You just go around back. I'll smooth this all over."

Me, "Alright, but I'm not apologizing to anybody."

So, we play. And apparently, it's fine. After our set I

run into Mark and his wife. We all apologize to each other and the whole incident is water under the bridge. We get drunk and dance the night away. I have very vague recollections of the end of the evening, but Jimi was kind enough to remind me of what stupid shit I did next. I'm in the middle of the party, drunk, yelling, "This is a good motherfuckin' party! I'm gonna have another motherfuckin' beer. I'm motherfuckin' drunk! Woo!" Jimi ushers me and the other guys out to the rental. We head back to the motel. The room is in my name, so there are more people this evening that I deal with in an inappropriate manner.

The next morning I wake up in the motel with an appropriate size hangover for the amount I drank on the previous day. I shower, we pack our stuff into the rental. I go back up to the room for an idiot check. Make sure we haven't left anything. We have not, but I notice that the toilet is running. It's been running the whole time we've been in this room. So, like the good citizen of the world that I am, I decide I will partake in the altruistic act of fixing this crapper. I pull the lid off the upper tank and peer inside. Looks totally normal except, of course, for the two fluorescent colored dildos in there. One white, one pink. The pink one is impeding the stopper. It can't close all the way so the toilet just continues to run and run. They were the kind of dildos with suction cups at the the base of them. You know, classy ones. I run out to the balcony, "Hey guys, come back up here for a second, there's something you gotta see.

Guys, "What? We need to go."

Me, "Just for a second, come on."

After they get an eyeful and snap some photos I move the dildos around so the tank can fill. I leave the dildos in there. We drive back to New York City.

-GRACELAND TOO-

Sorry folks, most of you guys probably missed this one. Truly thee greatest tour of a person's estate you could dream of going on. Of course I'm using the term estate loosely here. I'm talking about Paul McClouds house in Holly Springs, MS.

Let's start at the beginning. It's *The Mirrors* reunion tour. We start in Houston of course, because that is where everybody else in the band still lives. First gig, I'm gonna guess, is in Houston, unless the last gig was there. Either way the first out of town gig was Jackson, MS. Sam, and his girlfriend Kate, and Roadhouse's girlfriend Liz, tag along for the first few dates. I had heard about *Graceland Too* on *Gris Gris* tours when we were in Memphis. I think somebody brought it up at the Jackson show.

In a nutshell, *Graceland Too* is a house in a small town that is pink. Not the town, the house. There are statues of lions on either side at the top of the front steps. I believe there were columns too, but that doesn't mean there was. It's a proper southern home. The place is full of Elvis memorabilia. Records, pictures, etc...... That's not what's great about the place. Paul McCloud is the show. People tell us, "You can go anytime 24/7, 365 and this crazy hoarder will give you a tour of his shitty house. You can bring in beer and drink while you're taking the tour."

Sold. We're going from Jackson to Memphis, and Holly Springs isn't a big detour. It's a short travel day either way, plenty of time to stop and check this out.

We pull into Holly Springs. Me and Chad go into a *Subway* to get a sandwich and directions. This was before

the days of smart phones and all that bullshit. We pull into town only knowing this house is located there. No directions. We are told, "Just go to Holly Springs and ask anybody, they'll steer you in the right direction."

Chad, to the lady making our sandwiches, "Um, excuse me, do you know where a place called *Graceland Too* is?"

Hilarious older black lady, "Oh I know where that is. That crazy old man. First his wife left him, then his ugly ass son left him." She gives us directions. We drive into town and eventually find *Graceland Too*. It would have been hard to miss the place since the house is pink, and there isn't much of a town to get lost in in the first place.

We park and walk up the stairs to the house. Before we can knock Mr. McCloud opens the door. "You guys here for the tour? It's five dollars each, sign in here." We all sign into the guest book, or whatever you call one of those things.

Before any Elvis stuff, he starts in on the girls. I doubt this guy has gotten any pussy in decades. "You ladies have mothers? Aunts? Grandmothers? I can just go all the time. My wife told me they should send me to China. You know they got that stars, scars...."

One of us, "SARS?"

McCloud, "Yeah SARS. She said I could help re-populate China." Bullshit Paul, your wife was gone long before SARS showed up. While he speaks his dentures continually fall out of place. He consistently catches them with his lips, nudging them back into their spot across his gums.

He tells us of his son, Elvis Aaron Presley McCloud.

Apparently back in the 90's, if you showed up for a tour, half the time you would get McCloud's poor son. They worked in 12 hour shifts or something. I can't remember what bullshit he told us about where his son was now, maybe the service or something, but I am pretty positive his son turned 18 and got the fuck out of there and changed his name. I wander what dude is doing today? Right now.

Alright, on to Elvis. He brings us into a room with a bunch of photos and postcards and junk. There is a glass case with a 7" record inside it. "This record is priceless," he tells us. "Bill Clinton tried to buy it off me for fifty thousand dollars and I told him hell no. You know Tom Cruise's dog was here yesterday. Lots of famous people come here." Yeah Tom Cruise's dog is pretty fucking impressive. He shows us the room with the "Member" photos. If you go to *Graceland Too* three times you become a member for life. You get a Polaroid taken of yourself wearing a leather jacket that McCloud provides, and then you join the others in the great walk in closet of memberdom. I believe the tour is also free from there on out.

He takes us into another room full of boxes and plastic storage containers. "I've recorded every appearance of Elvis on television for the last 20 years. Any mention of Elvis or anything like that, I have it all on VHS. Give me a date, any date. I have on file every mention of Elvis in the news ever." We give him a date. He pulls out a binder. Tells us what's up with the Elvis news that day. He shows us some things upstairs, but I can't recall what now. The backyard has been made to look like the set of *Jailhouse*

Rock. He has a fake electric chair in his garage. McCloud to Chad, "Come inside the garage and sit in the chair."

Chad to McCloud, "Uh uh, I ain't goin' in there."

McCloud probably said and did a bunch of other crazy shit that I just can't remember. I need to call Alan and get his take. I remember he kept a tour diary for the first like three days and then gave up, which is a shame cuz he's a good writer.

Anyways fast forward nine years, give or take, I bring *The John Brothers* to Mecca. Same thing if I remember correctly, McCloud's at the door before we can knock. We bring in a twelve pack. Jimi asks if it's alright if we drink beer during the tour. McCloud says, "Sure, that's fine, just don't spill any." Jimi cracks a beer and it immediately foams over onto McCloud's floor. McCloud kind of freezes for a second, giving Jimi the evil eye, then the tour begins.

This time McCloud is packing heat, carrying a gun around in his hand while he gives the tour, periodically saying to Arlo, "Here, hold my gun." Arlo would reach out his palm where the gun would be placed over and over again while McCloud pulls random shit out of drawers and piles to show us. Arlo just stands there with the gun sitting on his open palm like a waiter with a tray.

McCloud was definitely much more animated this time. He's constantly slapping Jimi and Arlo on the chest, all whilst giving a little whistle. This is how he gets their attention when he wants one of them to read some random shit out of one of his binders or old newspapers. He shows us scraps of carpet from the hotel room Elvis died in. According to him they are worth $50,000 a square inch.

He informs us that he has several yards of this crap. His grasp of fake statistics, monetary values, and dates is dizzying. He's obviously making all this shit up, but it is consistent inside of his own insanity. He shows us the "Untied Nations" he now has out back, which consists of a dozen or so US and Confederate flags. Jimi sits in the electric chair. (Who's the pussy now Chad?)

At one point McCloud, gun in hand, says to Arlo, "Open this drawer right here, there's something in there I want you to see." Arlo, with a revolver pointed at him, opens the drawer and pulls out a zip-lock bag full of women's underwear. "Open it up and smell that pussy," says McCloud. "Well go on. You know I got those panties from a Chinese girl that tried to break in here. She was built like a brick shit house, pretty face though. She snagged her panties on the razor wire out back, cut her pussy right open. Then her dog took a crap on my porch and I made her eat it."

I'm loving every second of this. I just stand there drinking *Busch Light* in the back of the line watching McCloud's crazy ass spout Elvis nonsense to my pals.

We played in Oxford, MS that evening. I tell my friend Johnny I took these guys to *Graceland Too*. Johnny says to me, "Man I took my whole family there last year, they were pissed at me for weeks."

Later that year Arlo tells me he read on the internet McCloud died. Apparently someone came into *Graceland Too* with a gun and tried to rob the place. Paul shot the guy and killed him. Two days later he had a heart attack and died. I'm bummed I never got to become a member. I was so close. I'm assuming his wife and son reappeared after his death, sold all that junk, and hopefully made a buck. Seems to me like they earned it.

-DAMON THE HEATHEN-

I moved into *The Ghost-town Gallery* in September of 2007. I had gotten kicked out of my place with Hoyt on 34th street for recording bands in my bedroom. The neighbor upstairs kept complaining. Chris Stroffolino got me the room in the warehouse. He's another Oakland character. Piano man, a real sweet dude. He played keys on a bunch of my stuff over the years and I recorded one of his albums.

I lived in that dump for almost 9 years. We had bedbugs twice. I slept in a tent in my room for around a year in total. I never used the kitchen for anything but to wash my dishes, which I kept in my room. I had a hot plate, mini fridge, microwave, toaster, and toaster oven all in my room. I had had roommates before and knew the kitchen and bathroom were always the biggest challenge. No way out of sharing the bathroom with twenty people, but I certainly wasn't gonna fuck with that kitchen. The floor of all the common areas in the place were constantly covered in a layer of old beer spillage and there was next to no heat in the winter. Even if you had a space heater there wasn't much sense in bothering to run it because the place wasn't insulated at all and the electric bill was crazy even without them. Here's another example of what the baseline operating level of cleanliness and repair was at the warehouse.

I woke up one night around four in the morning thinking I would shit myself. I did not. I ran to the bathroom, which was very far away from my bedroom, pulled down my boxer shorts and took a diarrhea shit into the toilet. Liquid shooting out of my asshole. Not pretty. I had an instant reaction to flush even though there is no reason to. Normally I would be shitting at a house, apartment, or some regular place that a human being should be taking a shit at. My brain was so twisted and fucked up at this point that I couldn't even process this, so I instantly did the courtesy flush. I'm sitting there, head in my hands, in the middle of the night zoning out, and all of a sudden I have a sensation in my balls. Why are my balls wet? I look down. The toilet starts to overflow. My cock and balls are submerged in the diarrhea water! Mine and God knows who else's. I jump up, grab the plunger from behind the toilet, and start mashing it into the shit soup. After 30 seconds or so the toilet is unclogged and the water finally spirals down. I immediately jump in the shower and throw away my boxers. I never got back to sleep that night.

The man in charge of *The Ghost-town Gallery* was a hood named Damon, or at least that's how he'd like to be remembered. Damon, not the sweetest dude on earth, was a polarizing figure for sure. Peter used to work the door at *The Ruby Room* near the lake in Downtown Oakland when Damon was a bartender there. Peter said one night, when it was raining, Damon was trying to fuck one of the other bartenders and Peter was waiting for a cab home. Damon was getting a little perturbed at how long the cab was taking. "Hey Peter, you call a cab man?"

Peter says, "Yeah, I called them."

Ten minutes later, "Hey Peter, your cab's here." Peter steps outside into the pouring rain, no cab. He turns around to go back inside and Damon has locked the door.

Peter can see him fucking the other bartender doggy style against the bar. Peter walks home in the rain.

Now Damon is not a bad guy. Shit, I wouldn't have had my recording studio in that warehouse for nine years if it wasn't for him. Damon's just an asshole. He ruffled a lot of feathers in his decade or so in Oakland. He's a motherfucker who gets shit done is what he is. He would always be opening a new bar or restaurant or venue in town. I was always trying to figure out how this crazy, coke head, son of a bitch was accomplishing all this. Some people would say he's a sociopath, that's how. I called him that one time when he was bitching me out for nothing. I saw him the next day and he said he had to look that shit up on the internet. I figured out how to deal with Damon pretty quickly. Avoid his ass when he's in a bad mood and pay the rent on time, not exactly rocket science.

That motherfucker always had my back though, and not for really any reason that I could figure out. I moved into a tiny room with a low ceiling, which doesn't mean fuck all to me cuz I'm short. That room was next to a giant room with high ceilings full of trash and bike parts. Over the course of a couple months I got rid of the trash and replaced it with my recording equipment and what-not. My rent was $450 when i moved in. After two months Damon comes by and tells me, "Rent's $500." On the first of the next month, with no warning mind you, he informs me, "Rent's $550." January '08, "Looks like you got two rooms Greg, Rent's $750." My rent stayed at that until we all got evicted in June of 2016. I never said shit, I kept my head down and paid the rent. It was a steal no matter what, and you gotta know how to pick your battles if you're gonna survive in this world.

My neighbor upstairs, again just like my last place, was constantly complaining about the noise. I have always had a rule, always, to only record for six hours at a time between noon and 8pm. Rules get broken when they have to be broken, but that's my normal routine. Wont wake anybody up, wont keep anybody up. Or at least anybody that has a job and can complain about noise. Chris something (not Stroffolino) was the baritone sax player in Damon's band. To this day that instrument is completely ruined for me, all I hear is *Damon and The Heathens* when I hear that shit. Peter had a great impersonation of Damon, "YOU HEAR ME!?"

Chris would spend a large portion of his day, God bless him, giving it to his old lady upstairs, who was very vocal. I was recording bands all the time back then and invariably someone would be doing something quiet, like a vocal overdub, and the fucking would start. Loud as shit. This is the cunt that's telling me to keep it down. I probably have that bitch's fake ass orgasm in the background of at least a few old reels of tape.

People I'd be recording ask me, "What is that? What is that sound?"

I say, "Just ignore it."

One guy I recorded asks, "What does this chick do for a living? Just hang out and get nailed all day?"

Chris complains to Damon after I had been there for a few months. Damon, "Listen man, Greg's just trying to run his recording studio down there. This is a warehouse for artist's and musicians. If you wanna get married or whatever, move out to Berkeley or the suburbs or something." Now this might have been an altruistic gesture or a hint of integrity on Damon's part, or maybe they had an ongoing feud, I have no idea, but Chris and his old lady moved to Berkeley the next month. I got a new neighbor that couldn't say shit cuz I was now the old tenant. Damon got me to show off when he was trying to rent a room to some new sucker, "Greg Ashley's down here with his studio," and everybody else in the warehouse got........

Damon was definitely a tough bastard. At some point in the three years that he had the lease on the place before I moved in, he fell off the roof and was impaled by a spike on the gate next door. This, I'm gonna guess, happened sometime in 2006, back when the phone company was still bothering to repair pay phones. Before almost everyone on the planet had a smart phone, and pay phones still got used once in a blue moon. There was one on our block of San Pablo and it was used constantly. It was located at the very northeast corner of the building. Whoever had the misfortune of occupying the room in that corner of the building would be constantly woken in the night by people talking on this phone. Damon was living in this room at the time of the incident.

Damon's in the kitchen one morning having coffee with some friends, recovering from his night of interrupted, spotty sleep, when he gets the bright idea to cut the phone line. So he climbs up on the roof and assesses the situation. He can't quite reach the line with his wire cutters, so he has to grab onto the decorative piece that is sticking up from that corner of the warehouse. He says he tested what he calls "the cap-stone", and it felt solid. He thought it was made out of limestone or something. So he puts his weight on it, leans out to cut the line and the fucking thing breaks off. He falls from the roof of the warehouse head first toward the sidewalk. He lands on the gate to the lot next door and a spike on it goes right through his left thigh. Luckily it didn't hit his femoral artery, but he is impaled on the fence hanging upside down next to the pay-phone.

It's around 10AM and the block is already in full swing. The crack heads and hookers are out doing their thing and he is hanging there by his leg bleeding all over the ground. He says one lady comes by, looks at him and starts chanting, "There's a white boy stuck on the fence! There's a white boy stuck on the fence!" She's trying to start a neighborhood chant or a rallying call or something. He says he can see his bone through the blood that's gushing out of his leg. Somehow this crazy motherfucker, I guess due to the fact that he is in shock and nobody is willing to help him, lifts himself up and slips himself off of the spike. He falls to the ground and lands on his back, in the lot next door, right next to a cactus.

So he's lying there with a hole in his leg squirting blood everywhere, trapped behind this padlocked fence. He's pleading with the people on the other side, "Call an ambulance! Please call an ambulance, I think this is bad."

One crack whore takes a good hard look at him and says, "Oh, you are fucked up! I gotta go get a beer." She actually left cuz she had to go get a beer. Damon was apparently number two on the list when it came to her priorities that morning.

Eventually one of the hoods from over on Mead street

comes by and sees what's happening. He's wearing an extra large white dress shirt with bedazzled sequins on it and shit. He says to Damon, "Man you're losing blood man, you're losin' a lotta' blood." Damon sees the guy start to unbutton his shirt and then hand it through the fence. "Man, this is my favorite fucking shirt."

Guy did Damon a solid, might have saved his life. Damon ties his leg off and the entire shirt gos red almost instantly. Eventually a fire truck and an ambulance show up, cut the lock to the gate, shoot him up with morphine, and rush him to Highland Hospital in East Oakland. Damon lives.

I'd always wondered about Damon's life before he became my landlord. I had heard snippets of little stories about his 20s from friends of his from Detroit. Apparently Damon was this kind of awkward pot head with a fro that used to DJ a bunch and set up shows and parties. By a twist of fate I was introduced to a guy that grew up with Damon in Indiana. His name is Seth. He used to sing for a band called *John Wilkes Booze*. My old band *The Mirrors* actually played with them way back in 99' or 2000 in Houston. I remember I kept their CD for years. It might even be in a box somewhere with other bits of my extraneous junk.

So many degrees of separation had to come together for this chance meeting to occur. Julia in Austin, who I dated long distance from November 2015 to the end of 2017, introduced us. Seth and Julia knew each other from Knoxville, TN, where Julia grew up. Seth had moved there from Lafayette, IN, for a couple years in the early 2000s. They were both in garage bands. At the time I was introduced to Seth he was living in San Francisco with his girlfriend. They have since moved and I don't know where dude is now. Julia was visiting me from Austin and she called him up. As me and Seth got to talking I realized who he was and that our bands had played together in the past. Then he told me where he was from and I asked him, by chance, if he knew a Damon from there. Turns out they were roommates when they were younger. What the fuck!?

Anyways onto his Damon story. Seth and Damon were roommates, I think, in the late 90s. They would waste away their afternoons drinking beer and watching talk shows like *Springer, Sally Jesse Raphael, Geraldo, Jenny Jones, and The Danny Bonnaduchi Show* (You know, the bass player from The Partridge Family). Damon was hell bent on getting on one of these shows. He wanted to, "Fuck one of them up."

My old drummer Jamie's mom Joan, the stripper from the *Ronnie The Cowboy in San Francisco* story, had been on *Jenny Jones* before. We saw the episode on VHS over at Jamie's on his 18th birthday. Joan and her boyfriend Josh were flown to Chicago and put up in a four star hotel for the duration of the taping. They were given loose scripts that said essentially, "Josh wants Joan to quit stripping," which was bullshit, I think he loved the fact that she was a stripper. Damon wanted a piece of this action, you see. So what does he do? He proceeds to call every talk show that comes on in the afternoon for a week or two telling them exactly what they want to hear.

During commercials and at the end of all these programs there are messages that come up on your television screen saying things like, "Do you have a sexual relationship with your pet hamster? Are you tired of taking your hermaphrodite teen to the abortion clinic after they have impregnated themselves? Is your dog a racist?" Now anybody could have got on that one, we all know dogs are notoriously racist. "If so, please call us at 1 (800) 555-5555."

Damon leaves messages with all the big ones. So many so that when he does get a call back from *The Danny Bonnaduchi Show* he has to feel out the producer on the phone for a few minutes before he can figure out which bullshit story he told them. Eventually he figures it out. It's something along the lines of, "Your significant other is cheating on you," or vise versa, or probably both. Damon is in. He gives the producer his info and the info of his new girlfriend. He has only been seeing this girl for a few weeks and has not run this by her in the least bit, if at all.

He calls his girlfriend, "Hey babe we're gonna be on TV! *The Danny Bonnaduchi Show*."

"I'm not going on there with you. My grandmother watches that show. You're fucking crazy." They break up. Damon is not fazed in the least bit, he's getting on that fucking show. Damon calls an ex-girlfriend that agrees to go with him. He doesn't bother to update the producers over in Chicago, he just tells his ex-girlfriend to say her name is whatever the other ex-girlfriend's name is. She is fine with that. Then he decides he wants Seth to go with them. Damon calls the producers and some how finagles another room and flight for his buddy.

So now they are off to Chicago and their appearance on *The Bonnaduchi Show*. Seth is seated in the studio audience. Damon and ex-girlfriend are ushered back stage.

According to Seth, Damon takes the stage first, recites whatever story the producers gave him, and then it's time for home-girl's appearance. She comes out yelling and talking shit, they mix it up for a bit and then........ the moment Damon has been waiting for. The part of the script he has written for himself. Girlfriend says, "And the worst part about all of it is, that every time we get in a fight you piss yourself." Damon, at this moment, pricks a water balloon hidden in his pocket wetting his crotch. Everybody goes fucking nuts. People are laughing and hollering and bagging on him all throughout the studio audience. The producers love it. At least for now.

After the taping him and ex-girlfriend are back stage filling out some final paperwork when the producers realize that the person Damon has brought to the taping is not the person they have in their documents. They need their IDs or something to that effect, and that is when they notice the discrepancy. They immediately separate Damon, Seth, and Ex. Seth says the producers of the show take him into a small room and begin to interrogate him about what he knew and when he knew it. Seth didn't know shit. He knew what Damon was capable of, but wasn't clued in to any of Damon's plans for the show. He was as in the dark as the rest of the studio audience. The producers of *The Danny Bonnaduci Show* end up filing a lawsuit against Damon for tens of thousands of dollars because they can't air the episode they just taped without the consent of the person who's name they have been using for his girlfriend. For months after this Damon has the tenacity to continually call and harass the producers of the show for a copy of the tape. He tells them he is in therapy and that his shrink thinks it would be therapeutic for him to see it. And according to Seth, Damon ends up getting them to send him a tape! Fucking Damon...... I'm assuming the lawsuit was eventually dropped. It's not like Damon would have had any assets or money for those people to take from him.

When I met Seth, Damon had already moved back to the Midwest following our eviction from the warehouse. But I did hang out with Damon earlier this year in Indiana when I was on tour. I asked him about the whole thing. He corroborated the story but didn't know what had happened to the tape. Man I wish I could see that fucking tape.

-WEST OAKLAND-

Dating Jess was the best. Except when it wasn't, and that was always my fault. I'd black out and do something fucked up. Say some fucked up shit to her, or someone else, or some group of people. I can be a mean drunk. After she had seen my capacity to do this on numerous occasions she started to try to put me in my place, get me to stop drinking before I blacked out and turned into a monster. Trying to get an alcoholic to stop drinking while they are still at all coherent is pretty much an exercise in futility.

Earlier this year we were getting wasted together and she put The Club on my truck and took my keys. This was to stop me from driving to the liquor store to get more vodka at 1AM. Well I had another set of keys to my truck. Not to the church unfortunately, and not to The Club that was on the steering wheel. So I decide fuck it, I can drive this thing down San Pablo with The Club on. It's a straight shot. Not really. I didn't realize the turning radius would be, to say the least, a bit wider with that Club on the steering wheel. I back out onto San Pablo and attempt a u-turn. It is a very wide u-turn, one that ends up taking me through the little parking lot of the taco stand across the street and then over the median of San Pablo, which is a three foot tall mound of dirt. I land right in the middle of Mead street right as an Oakland cop car passes by. I literally do this right in front of the cops. They definitely see me jump the median, and The Club is sticking out the window. I just sit there dumbfounded thinking well, this is it. This is the day I finally get busted driving drunk.

175

Cop, from the squad car asks me, "What the hell are you doing?"

"I don't know."

"Do you live around here?"

"Yeah I just live around the corner."

"Well leave your truck there and you can deal with it in the morning."

"OK." No argument here, what the fuck? I love this fucking town. You can't get arrested for shit if you're white.

I was doing coke in front of *The Nightlight* on Broadway one New Years and an Oakland cop rolls by just as I'm doing a bump. Key in nostril, I make eye contact with the officer. He just fucking waves. Happy New Year fuckers! I wish Oakland would never change and it could always be my home, but that's just not the way the world works I suppose.

Anyways, back to me and Jess. My blacking out is actually what got us together. One Sunday me and the boys in *The John Brothers Piano Company* play *The Boot and Shoe*, do our normal thing. It's off to *The Alley*, coke and booze. I black out, come to, I'm in the park by the lake eating Jess's pussy out. I just remember being at the bar, maybe going outside for a smoke and then bam! I'm in the park. Apparently I was bemoaning my loneliness and Jess was consoling me. I did something like asked her if she wanted to get out of there. After that we walk to *The Ghost-town*, run into Damon and some other fools, do a bunch of coke and then go to my room to screw.

This is all great and all, except for the fact that this is John's girlfriend. This was probably one of the most despicable things I've ever done in my life. I betrayed my friend. One of my best friends. John had kind of moved himself into Jess's house after they started dating. Something you do when you are a homeless musician. They had only been dating a few months. Me and Jess dated for over a year, broke up for a year or two, liked each other's company so much that we dated again for somewhere between six and nine months, then broke up again. That, by no means, makes this OK, but I can't help it, I'm making excuses for myself. Jess is still one of my best friends. I know we'll always be friends, well as long as I can stay off the sauce.

We had to come clean to John after a few days. It was terrible. We were going to LA for a series of three gigs the Tuesday after that Sunday. The plan was all five of us pile into my car and we drive down to LA together. A piano, drums and bass amp were being provided for the shows so no reason to waste the money on gas to take John's van. This motherfucker, without consulting any of us, takes Jess and himself in his van to his parent's house in southern California on Monday, then meets us at the gig on Tuesday. They show up and it's Jess, John, John's folks, and his sister who was dating Arlo at the time. What a fucking nightmare I've created for myself. I have to look John, his mom, and his dad in the eye and make polite conversation, all while knowing what I have done.

First night we played it off pretty cool I suppose. Night ended with me, John, and Jess sitting on the corner of Sunset and whatever polishing off a bottle of whiskey in the wee hours.

Day two, not so much. I'm sitting by the pool at the

hotel drinkin' a beer. Jess comes over and sits on the pool chair next to me. I ask her, "You wanna get out of here?"

"Yes." Me and Jess take off by ourselves and do our thing.

Day three, we have to come clean and we do. John was so hurt. I felt terrible, Jess did too. He took off to his folks place in the desert right after the gig. Jess rode back with us in my car. What can I say we were in love. I still love her, always will. I still hate myself for how it all happened though. It's shameful to say the least.

When we dated we both did what you would consider shameful things to each other, at least in the realms of monogamy that is. We compared notes and we each cheated on the other three times during round one. Round one ended when I hooked up with my next girlfriend, Julia while recording Wes Coleman at a studio near the town of Tornillo in West Texas. Julia played drums in Wes's band. Or sometimes she did. Wes always had a rotating cast of players.

I get back to California and tell Jess right away that I have fallen in love with another women etc....... She says, "Holy shit, I've been cheating on you too! I started seeing this guy while you were gone."

I say, "Great!" We get drunk together, everything's cool.

Now to the story at hand. I know I am kind of all over the place here. I've told you, we always had the best time together, still do. Many nights, back then, we would wander the streets of West Oakland. We'd explore the abandoned train station. We'd have fires in her back yard, burning anything combustible from the neighborhood we could find. We fucked in the house next door that was in the process of being built. I think we did it in what would later become the neighbor's bathroom. We'd climb into the freeway catwalks in the MacArthur maze, and smoke crack. We were having little kid adventures as adults and it was great! Especially since we were high on coke, weed, and booze all the time. It was pretty amazing to be fucked up suspended hundreds of feet in the air watching traffic fly by this way and that on the freeways above and below. The whole catwalk would be shaking like a leaf while we sat contemplating our life together.

One morning we went grocery shopping at *Trader Joe's*. Of course we buy a case of pinot grigio *Charles Shaw*. We get home, put up the groceries and start in on the wine. We go down to the lake and drink there. We wander around the neighborhood up the hill. We find someone's left over crap, that has moved, on the side of the street. Turns out it was our friend Zach's stuff, but that's irrelevant. He leaves some books, a cabinet, and a bag of pennies. We take the pennies. We head back toward the lake and stop at the fountain. There's a group of black teenagers sitting on the round marble seat that encircles the fountain. They're hangin' out drinkin' 40s. We pull up with our warm, dry white wine. We don't give a fuck, we've been drinking it like that all day. We're pretty toasted. I plop the bag of pennies down on the edge of the fountain and start tossing them in. "Make a wish foundation motherfuckers. Make a fucking wish!"

Jess starts throwing pennies in and wishing too. One black kid starts to gather the pennies like he's gonna collect enough of them to actually buy something. Then this crazy black girl grabs the pennies from him. "Get your hands off my wishes!" He backs off, then she goes on an amazing tirade. "I wish my dad wasn't so fuckin' old. I wish I never fucked a nigga'." etc....... Jess has footage of this from her phone somewhere.

One night we were wandering the streets of what is called The Lower Bottoms, the farthest west you can go in Oakland. That's where she lives. We're getting fucked up, walking her dog Batty. Of course we need a couple beers for our walk, so we stop into this liquor store on 9th and Willow. The place is just a tiny cube, like the size of a bedroom or something. I'm high as shit on weed. There's always a bunch of people partying in front of this store. Sometimes I would park by it back when I worked optometry in San Francisco. It's four or five blocks away from West Oakland BART. There'd be fools drinking in front of that place at 8 in the morning. We were there about 9pm that night I'd say.

Anyways, I go in and Jess stays outside with the dog and all the crazy black motherfuckers gettin' crunk. There's three chicks at the counter yelling and carrying on, but in a good way. They're just drunk or don't give a shit that they're making a scene. It's typical for pretty much any liquor store in Oakland. I walk past them and stare into the beer cooler. I figure I'll wait till they leave before I bother going up to the counter.

So I'm just staring into the cooler like I'm trying to make a decision on what I'm gonna purchase, even though I know full well what I'm getting. Two 24 ounce cans of *Coors Light*. Eventually they leave so I open the cooler and grab the cans. Then this other dude comes in and buys a pint of *Taka*. He asks the old Arab guy behind the counter for a receipt. It seemed like he needed it to prove to whoever sent him to the store that he wasn't cheating them for the vodka or something. That's all I could figure anyways. The old man says no. Dude asks again, "Come on, I need a fucking receipt."

Old man says, "No, get out."

Dude reaches across the counter. It didn't really seem like he was trying to punch the old man, just grab him or some shit. All of a sudden two young guys, probably the old man's kids or nephews or whatever, jump out of the stockroom and one grabs a giant can of chick peas and hits dude over the head with it. Other guy runs over and locks the door. All hell breaks loose outside. All the black folk outside that were partying start banging on the glass windows of the store and chanting "Let him go, let him go!"

I'm standing there with my beers thinking, "Oh fuck." I slink down the back isle in the very rear corner of the store and hide like a little bitch with my beers. Jess is outside with Batty freaking out cuz I'm trapped in the store and a fucking riot is about to break out.

Eventually the pigs show up. The store is swarming with them. There's six or seven cops in there. They cuff the guy that reached across the counter. He's bleeding out of his head. They place him on the ground in front of the door. They don't do shit to the guy that beat him over the head with a can of peas. I'm standing in the back isle with my beers, just kind of wandering what the fuck to do. Nobody seems to notice me.

Eventually I walk up to the register. "Can you ring me

up?" Old man rings me up. So now I'm standing there double fisting my *Coors* and I can't get out of the store cuz the exit is blocked by the bleeding guy. I walk up to one of the cops, "Hey uh, can you move him? I'm trying to get out of here."

Cop looks at me, "Wait, you were in here the whole time?"

"Yeah."

"What happened in here? What did you see?"

"Well the guy over there bought something and wanted a receipt for it, and the guy behind the counter wouldn't give him one. Then the guy on the ground there reached across the counter and these two guys jumped out of the back and hit him over the head with a can of peas."

"What's your name? Where do you stay at?" I give him my info. Where do I stay at? What am I, a fucking wigger? They move dude and I get the fuck out of there. Me and Jess go out to the tracks and drink our beers.

Now I never heard from the cops or anything. I'm assuming nothing ever came of the whole fiasco. If that old fuck had just given dude a receipt this whole thing could have been avoided. It was just another situation of two or more unreasonable people in a room together getting into it. Stupid shit happens, violence ensues, and the cops get involved.

I can't really decide in my mind if there's a side I take in the whole matter. It was pretty excessive to hit that poor bastard over the head with a can of peas, but then again, he shouldn't have tried to grab the old man. Also the old man should have just given him a receipt. It's not that hard, and the guy kind of has the right to one after he makes a purchase. Like I said before, the cops didn't do shit to the two younger guys for assaulting that guy. Then again it is their store, and that guy's fucking with their old man. Anyways, I don't shop there anymore.

I've gotten into quite a few dicey situations where I live in West Oakland. Always due to my drug and alcohol abuse. If you don't fuck around buying street drugs or wandering around wasted after dark, you'll get by without too much trouble. Just don't make eye contact with anyone, and watch the fuckers lurking in the shadows.

I followed these simple rules I made for myself for a decade and remained fairly anonymous in my neighborhood. Then I started to buy crack off the street with some frequency this last summer. Big fucking mistake. I stopped doing that, but now motherfuckers know my name, "Yo Greg! What you looking for? Let's smoke." That's subsided now and I've returned to my anonymity, but it was pretty fucking annoying for a couple months.

I've been robbed at gunpoint twice. Once buying crack in the tent city under the freeway by where I live, and once inside my home, the church. Here's how you find a rock in the middle of the night when you don't know where to go because your normal honest drug dealers have all turned in for the evening.

First, you walk to the liquor store to find the prostitutes that hang on the corner working all night. "Greg, what's up? You wanna party?"

"No, I'm looking for a rock. You know where to get some shit?"

"Here, give me your money, I'll take care of it." This

works, yes, but you end up having to give, or at least smoke some of your crack with a prostitute on the corner.

If the hookers aren't chillin' by the liquor store you go to the tent city under the freeway and just wander around until somebody asks you what you're looking for. Sometimes motherfuckers just take your money and never return, or sometimes you get ushered into a tent. Either way you get fucked about 50% of the time if not more. This option is certainly the last resort.

One time I went into a tent and bought crack from a crazy woman. We smoked together and then I was gonna take off and I guess I said or did something she didn't like, I can't remember. I'm gathering my shit and she starts yelling, "Oh, hell no! Fucking crazy ass white boy. Yo T., get the mace! Come in my tent!" Fuck this, I'm looking for the zipper to get the fuck out of there. All of a sudden T. enters with a gun. I hand over the money in my wallet, maybe 20 or 30 bucks, can't remember. Not a super big loss, I suppose, since I didn't get shot.

The other time I got robbed I don't wanna talk about. I lost Two grand and a hundred bars of Xanax. Enough said...........

-THE WAREHOUSE-

So I've told you guys a little about some of the characters from *The Ghost-town Gallery*. Damon, *The John Bros*, Stroffolino, but let's see if I can remember some of the other fools that inhabited that dump. Joachim, who lived there, referred to the place as a dormitory for drug addicts. Not too far from the truth.

There were the junkies, Ben and Matt. I had my spell snorting heroin with them occasionally. Well, I'd snort it, they'd shoot it. Ben taught me how to cook black tar heroin so I could drip it down my nose. It's not a powder you can snort like china white or cocaine. It's a gross fucking tar, nasty stuff. They were shooting that shit into their veins. Hardcore man. We scored powder heroin twice, the rest of the time it was tar. That's the shit you can get in this neighborhood on the street.

They didn't like to shoot dope in front of me. I don't think most junkies do like to shoot up in public. You ever meet a junkie at the bar? Not usually, depends on the kind of places you hang out at, and I do hang out at those kinds of places. I've never seen it though. They're a secretive bunch, junkies.

You see somebody bust out a syringe in the crapper of some dive and everybody's gonna shit, "Dude, why can't you just use drugs like a normal person?" Now you pull out a fucked up sandwich bag, full of a chalky-white powder that smells like gasoline and stick that up your nose, nobody's even gonna bat an eye. Shit, they'll probably start begging your for a bump.

I watched them both shoot dope maybe once, but that

was it. I remember seeing Ben shoot up under his balls one time cuz he had run out of veins.

They were both great musicians. They both played on my Cohen album. Ben would be on top of the world when he got his fix. Skipping down the halls of *The Ghost-town* and shit, singin' a song. I brought him to Austin to play drums for me at *SXSW* one year. Poor fucker. The Suboxone, or Methadone, or whatever he scored to get through the trip just wasn't getting the job done. He was pretty miserable on both the flight there and back.

Once we got to Austin and got settled in at Sam's place, we quickly realized he was gonna have to get some real shit. I told Sam he had the flu instead of, "I brought a junkie into your house old friend. Great to see ya, let's have a beer, catch up on old times. Oh the guy crying and puking and shitting himself there on your couch. That's just my new pal Ben. He's cool, you'll really like the dude."

So on day two, while Sam is at work, Ben gets a hold of someone in Oakland, who knows somebody, that knows someone in Austin that can score dope. We borrow Sam's car, and in the afternoon we head north on I-35 towards downtown, through the hell of Austin traffic during *South-by*. We pick up some girl that has us take her back to the south-side of town. I'm driving, she's directing. This is all looking very familiar to me.

Crusty chick, "OK, so left here, right here, and do you know these apartments over here?"

"Yeah I know where we're at." Ben buys smack from the crusties that live a couple doors down from Sam. Ben is stoked, understandably so.

I regale this story to Sam a couple years later. His response is, "Thanks dick."

I say, "Sorry dude, the guys a good drummer. That's hard to find."

"I hung out with those crusties once. They were blown away by my shit-hole apartment. They told me I was living large!" He was not. Sam worked at *Kinko's* and drove his dead grandmother's piece of shit *Buick*.

Let's see who else inhabited this den of sin. There was a white rapper, slash skater, named Jesse that sold ecstasy. Everyone loved ecstasy, who doesn't. He moved out when Damon laid into him for intruding on his practice and trying to freestyle over Damon's music. I still hang with Jesse every once in a while, good guy.

There was a wigger, who's last name was, I shit you not, Wigger. He never wanted to give me the five bucks I had to collect every month for the internet. I had that shit in my name and it sucked. A lot of people in the warehouse would be bitches about throwing in. Like this was some elaborate scheme I had cooked up to make five bucks a month off every motherfucker that lived there. I would have gladly given somebody else my five bucks. I was just collecting what it costs. Damon ended up beating Wigger's ass in the hallway and Wigger moved out. It was a beautiful thing.

There was Anthony, who I started referring to as Tony Ching Chang in later years. He's half Korean, half Mexican. He lives in Seattle now, or at least I think he does. We used to hang out and take Vicodin while drinking whiskey and playing *Nintendo. Mike Tyson's Punch Out* was his game. He slayed at that shit. I watched him beat that fucker at least once.

Then you got Damon again. Damon loved him some cocaine. So did the Johns. Booze was my drug of choice, though I dabbled in all of it. I loved cocaine, but just the right balance between coke and booze. Too much booze, you could regain control with a line or two. Too much coke and you could come back down with the sauce, and everybody loved to have a drink or two while they were getting stoned.

Naomi certainly loved a drink or two. She was this crazy British chick that, big surprise, drank like a motherfucker. I helped her get her room at *The Ghost-town* because she was pretty and liked to booze it up. The fact that she was totally insane didn't seem to bother me at the time, and it certainly didn't bother Damon. He rented her a room. He knew that bitch was crazy, we both did, but we both wanted to sleep with her and we both knew that would probably be a really bad idea, but that's the way the world works. Naomi was fun though, maybe not when she was blacked out, but most people aren't fun when they're blacked out, so she gets a pass there. Blacked out or not, it was usually fairly entertaining to get wasted with a cockney chick that says cunt a lot. It's just fun getting drunk with hot girls. That's why bars and people exist.

The most famous resident of the warehouse was Brontez, My favorite of the gays. Last time I saw him was over on Telegraph, "Hey Greg, I put you in my book. I fucked all you rock 'n' roll white boys." Let's not get carried away Brontez, we got wasted together and cuddled once while commiserating our standing in the world as middle age garage rock nobodies. I don't remember it going further than that.

Brontez is a funny motherfucker. He technically lived next door at *Sugar Mountain*, but it's all the same building, just sectioned off in these fucked up ways. *Ghost-town* was on the north side and included the whole top floor. *Sugar Mountain* was on the south-side, and there was an enormous grow-op in the rear of the building.

One time we were having a show at *Ghost-town* and I walk through the front room while Brontez is going on a tirade about being tired of sucking dick. I think, "This is fucking hilarious."

Brontez to the room, "I'm not sucking anymore dick. I've been sucking dick my whole life and I'm through with that shit."

Me, "Hey Brontez, would you suck my dick?"

"I'll suck you dry any day of the week baby. You just say the word." I decided I'd keep that in my back pocket in case I ever got curious, but I haven't taken him up on it yet. I'm not homophobic, I don't give a fuck. I like a good blowjob just as much as any guy, and I'm sure it would be.

Another time we're all getting loaded in John's room and I run into Brontez in the hall, "Hey Brontez, come hang out with us fucker."

"OK." The room is small mind you. There is like two chairs, maybe a lazy boy, and John's bed to sit on. Then a table in the middle of the room that is covered in full, empty, and half drank beers, plus probably a mirror with cocaine on it. Everybody's got their seats and there's just one place left for Brontez to sit. On the bed, next to John.

John used to be a linebacker in high school. He's a big son of a bitch. But he's also from California, so I figure it's no big deal if I invite a fag into his room to drink with us. Brontez plops down on the bed. John starts to get this sort of uncomfortable look on his face. Classic. We're all drinking, just havin' a good old time, at least I thought so. Eventually Brontez kind of leans back on the bed for a yawn and stretch. John jumps up, "Oh hell no, Fuck no!"

Brontez jumps up knocking the table over, spilling all the drinks and cocaine. He goes screaming out of the room down the hall. I chase him, "Brontez! It's cool man, chill out."

John, "It's not fucking cool Greg. Not cool!" Shit, I spooned that dude in my bed, all Brontez was doing in John's was having a little yawn. It was getting late.

Oh man, and then there was Sean. What a crazy kid he was, in a good way. I've known Sean since he was 14 or 15, a long time. We first met when he hired me to record his band. I drove down to Southern California, where he's from, and we got to work. We do this in his grandmother's garage. I stayed in his family's house and crashed on their couch. I was there for a few days. I remember his mother saying to me, "Just please don't buy Sean any beer." Of course I did.

Then years later he shows up in Oakland with one of his buddies. They come to a show at the warehouse. Sean tells me, "We're moving up here man. We're scoping out places this week."

I say, "Cool, great." The night wears on and I guess Sean gets pretty hammered. He wanders out onto San Pablo Avenue late in the evening, looking for a place to buy a pack of smokes. Some crack whore directs him down an alley where three dudes with knives jump out of the shadows and steal his fanny pack with all his money and wallet shit in it.

Sean returns to the warehouse incensed, yelling crazy shit and just freaking out. I understand that reaction now, it sucks getting robbed. Back then, not so much. Sean and his friend leave right then and there to drive back to LA. They decide they're not moving to Oakland anymore.

Sean starts a band called *Cumstain*. They are great. Hilarious, ridiculous garage punk, and Sean puts on a stage show that's amazing. He wears nothing but a leopard print thong stuffed with a cucumber. I play some shows with them over the years down in Southern California and it's always a good time.

Sean drove an old cop car, it was so fucked. He got a bunch of parking tickets on it or something and it got towed. Sean goes to pick it up from the impound, pay the man. When he gets to the tow-yard, the gate is open. Sean sees his car and it's not too far in there. He makes a run for it. Steals his car from the impound lot. He said when he was pulling out, one of the employees sees what's going on and starts yelling at him. Sean drives away, fuck them. He heads home. Runs inside to hide because he's just realized the gravity of the situation at hand. Of course the police are there in minutes. They're not stupid. Well they are stupid, but they do have the address the car is registered to on file. Cop comes to the front door, "What the hell are you doing kid?"

Sean playing real dumb, "The gate was open, I saw my car, figured I'd take my car back." I can't recall what they did to him. I think he just ended up having to pay the fines and then whatever. The pigs went easy on him.

At some point in all of this insanity, he finally moves up to Oakland. He moves into *Sugar Mountain* so I see him pretty frequently. We hang out sometimes. Eventually he kind of chills out, quits drinking and gets a steady girlfriend, Erin. She's cool as shit. A real fucking fighter. You don't fuck with Erin.

Sean still has that piece of shit cop car when he moves to Oakland. He, of course, gets a million parking tickets on it again. Bullshit street sweeping tickets. Street sweeping does nothing but extort money from the poor. The streets in our neighborhood a covered in trash and needles no matter what the fucking city does. Sean's car gets booted. So Sean being Sean, just removes the boot. Then after he's got his tire back on the car he takes a look at the fine print on the boot, which contains talk of felony incarceration and fines. He figures he's pretty fucked. The car has a bunch of problems anyways. He doesn't have the money for the tickets and he can't get that fucking boot back over the tire.

He's parked on Athens Avenue right beside the warehouse. We were always up on the roof of *Ghost-town* partying and grilling and shit. It was great. You could have jumped off that roof and killed yourself on that car if you wanted to, but screw that. Sean's mindset, and all of ours is of course, fuck the police, and fuck the government. They're gonna go and auction that car for pennies on the dollar to some prick, and the money will just essentially vaporize. So he sets the boot against the wheel it was on, goes up on the roof with a cinder block, and repeatedly tosses it onto the car. He does this until the thing is just pretty much totally destroyed. I wish I was there to see it. I got to destroy a car in front of Jess's place one time. Taking an axe to the hood of an old beater really makes you feel alive.

Then there was Little Tony and Sox. They were a couple guys I knew from El Paso. I got them their room at the warehouse. Little Tony's real name was Antonio, and Sox's real name was Miguel. You see, every Mexican on the planet has four or five names. You have the Spanish version of their first name, the English version of it, their nickname, maybe a middle name, and their last name. Tony is short so that's a no-brainer. Sox got his nickname, supposedly, because when he said, "That sucks," or, "This sucks," it sounded like he was saying sox instead of sucks.

The two of them shared one room just like John and Thatcher, although I don't think they had any problems paying their rent. They both always had some shitty job at a grocery store or something, and they both DJ a bunch for extra cash and free drinks. Tony is one of the best Djs I know. "The fucking *Stones* dude, they're fucking bad!" Imagine that with a Mexican accent, it's way better. In fact, just imagine everything these two guys say with a Mexican accent.

I fucking love drinking with Tony. Neither of us drink anymore, and I still love hanging out with Tony, that's how cool this motherfucker is. He played drums in *SLVR* after Bronzini quit. He's probably my favorite rock 'n' roll drummer to play with. Our practices would always end with me and Tony staying up till the wee hours of the morning getting royally fucked up.

Damon has moved in upstairs from me during this time, I have no idea why. He would come down and turn off the stereo when me and Tony were half blacked out. Tony would talk mad shit to Damon, it was fucking hilarious, like watching a chihuahua bark at a pit bull. "Fuck you Damon, with your lame *Disneyland*, Dixieland jazz band. You Tom Waits wanna be bitch."

"Hey Tone, Tone, calm down. You guys aren't even listening to this music. You're like fucking zombies right now. Just go to bed, Jesus." Damon had a point I suppose.

Tony drank himself into the hospital and learned his lesson long before I did. He is like five or so years older than me though, so I guess there's really no difference. He went on a bender one time, that I believe ended with heroin and a bottle of *Ancient Age*. But I could have the details wrong. All I know is that some of the other residents of the warehouse found him puking up black shit in the hallway and they took him to Highland Hospital in East Oakland. Highland is the worst. This is where you end up if you've been shot or stabbed or impaled on a fence spike.

I go to visit Tony in the hospital, his roommate has gangrene or something from his lower legs down to his feet. Looked like crocodile skin. They've taken Tony's cap. Tony never took that fucking cap off, he would wear that thing into the shower. He slept in it. He lived in that hat. Tony is in that club of secret bald men that I am slowly joining myself. I've only seen Tony's head one other time, when he was passed out drunk. I took his cap off to, as Lars would say, "See what's under the hood." I had suspected, and my suspicions were correct. I'm in that hospital room thinking, "Man, just give Tony his hat back. Just give him his hat back."

Tony is curled up in the fetal position on the bed. "Greg, oh man, I'm so fucked up Greg." I give Tony this little video player I've loaded up with movies and music. I hope I put some *Stones* on there for him, I can't remember.

After this Tony cleans up his act and eventually moves back to El Paso. I think I stayed with him last time I went through there. I know we hung out and drank NA beer together.

I loved drinking with Sox too, I think he's still in Oakland. Last time I saw him, he was dating one of Jess's house mates, Chrystal. She's a piece of work, let me tell you. I love Chrystal, she's hilarious. Also from Houston. Didn't know her back in the day or anything, but I got to know her pretty well in Oakland. Last time I saw her was a couple years ago when Leonard Cohen died. There was a tribute show at the venue she worked at. I played, and a bunch of other people played. I was on one of my sober stints at the time.

I run into Chrystal and she is wasted. We're both in the crowd with all these somber people that are sort of mourning. Everyone is dead silent except for Chrystal. She's screaming and rocking out. People are shushing her and she is telling them to fuck off. "All these people have a stick up there ass. You wanna do some blow Greg?"

"OK." Why God, why?

And then in 2016 we all get evicted for nothing........

-EVICTION, DETOX, REHAB & SOME FLIGHTS FROM HELL-

I've been medically detoxed from alcohol somewhere around fifteen times in the last five years. Twice at a proper detox hospital, twice out-patient with my primary care physician, and I think four times in an emergency room. I've also detoxed myself seven or eight times at home using Xanax I bought off a drug dealer. That's pretty much the long and short of an alcohol detox. You replace the booze with a benzo-diazapam, then you wean yourself off the benzos slowly. If you do it too quick you'll have a seizure or a heart attack.

I've had four seizures in the last three years. First one was in Austin the month after we all got evicted from *The Ghost-town*. I had been drinking extremely heavily after we all got kicked out. I pretty much had a nervous breakdown.

I lived in that building for nine years. I had my home and business there. I always paid my rent not on time, but early. The landlord had been trying to get rid of us for over a year. He wanted to fix the place up and triple the rent, which he did. Damon was in a lawsuit with him. I could never get a straight answer from anyone as to when we would have to move, but I figured I would get at least a couple months notice and a settlement. I knew other people that had been evicted from their places by scum-bag landlords and they got thousands of dollars to move, and months to do it. I figured I'd been there for nine years so I'd have some time and some dough coming to me. Not the fucking case.

In the nine years that I lived in that warehouse we had six inspections from the fire department. The first five we passed with flying colors. Number six, when the landlord wants us gone, the fire inspector decides that a room has been built in an area that blocks a fire exit.

Now that room had been there all along, and there was never a problem. So now instead of money and time this is what we get. A notice from the city on the front door saying the building has been deemed by the fire department to be unsafe for habitation, and we have five days to vacate the premises.

This was two days before I was supposed to fly to France to do a two week tour of the country. It was all booked and my plane ticket was purchased of course. So I have two days to move my whole life to who the fuck knows where, and then leave the continent not knowing where I would live or work on my return. I lost it, started slamming straight vodka and crying like a bitch. My friends stepped in to help.

Somebody talks to Kenny who has the lease on the church and he tells them I can store my stuff in there until I figure things out. I take BART to SFO, I get my boarding pass, I walk up to my gate, I'm gonna be the last one to board the plane. I turn around and take BART back to Oakland, I can't do it. I can't leave the country with this hanging over my head. I keep drinking. Julia buys me a plane ticket to Austin, she's gonna take care of me. All my friends band together and move all my recording equipment and belongings into the church. I can never repay any of them for what they did for me. My friends have been saving me for years now. I'm blessed and I'm a fucking mess.

So now I'm in Austin in June, it's so fucking hot outside. I had had thoughts of moving back to Texas, but now I am remembering why I left this shit-hole state. I keep drinking. There is a liquor store that's a fifteen minute walk one way from Julia's and a gas station that's fifteen the other way.

One day Julia works and I keep trying to make it to the store. I walk halfway five or six times but the heat is killing me, and I'm weak as fuck from drinking so much. I give up. She calls me from the grocery store on her way home from work and asks me if I want anything. I say, "Please, please can you buy me a beer." She does. She gets home half an hour later or so and I help her in with the groceries. I should have just slammed that beer the second she got home. I'm helping her put everything away and the next thing I know, I'm in an ambulance with a chipped front tooth.

I stay in the hospital a day or two and then I'm fine. I even go to Ohio to play *The Blackout Fest*. Julia comes with me. She was so good to me and I know I put her through hell, treated her like shit.

I end up coming back to California and Kenny lets me make the church my home. I start recording bands there, things are going well. Julia is livid that I'm not moving to Texas. Eventually we break up. The next couple years are a roller-coaster ride of sobriety and drunkenness. I can stay sober for a month or two, or at most three, and then something derails me.

I finally make it to France in January of 2017. Me and Nico and the other French guys start recording what will become my next album. I drink a liter of shitty scotch everyday that I'm at Nico's studio in the French countryside. I have smuggled some Xanax with me and am taking that while I'm drinking instead of saving it for when I'm really gonna need it. You know, when I need to stop drinking. We get some great work done though, and I write songs with those guys. Something I have really never done. 99% of the time I write my songs alone, always have. They are hands down the best group of musicians I have ever played with. They have all been playing together since they were kids I think, so they know how to work off each other perfectly. They are all expert listeners, they never step on each other musically. They know how to leave sonic space like no-one I have ever played with. We spend ten days recording, then we are supposed to tour for ten days. I make it one day on tour and then lose it. I can't do the tour. They have to cancel the whole thing. I fucked up again.

We end up spending the next week or so in a freezing church from the 12th century that Manu's family owns. I just lie in a cot next to a space heater and shake and eat Gabapentin by the handful, praying I don't have another seizure. I don't.

The flight home is hell. I have to take an *Air Canada* flight to Montreal, then a four hour layover, then *United* or something else shitty to SFO. The complete travel time is 24 hours from door to door. We have to drive from Caen, in Normandy, to Paris first. That's like three hours or so. Then the flights, then my hour long BART ride home. What a nightmare.

I remember getting to Charles DeGaul in Paris and

picking up my boarding pass. The receptionist says, "Oh here, I can change your seat to an isle, that way you'll be more comfortable."

"Great," I think.

She puts me next to a 400 pound Hatian woman. That woman should definitely have been required to buy two seats. I had half a fucking seat. She knew how to make me fit though. She had the whole routine figured out. She had certainly done this many a time. I sit in that seat for two or three hours. It's a ten hour flight mind you, and my back is starting to kill me. I'm drinking as much as I can get my hands on to stay sane but finally I can't take it anymore. I get up and politely ask the stewardess, in the most diplomatic manner I could, if I could change seats.

"You see, I have a kind of situation with my seat, and I was wondering if it would be alright if I changed seats. I just don't have a lot of room in my current one."

Stewardess looks me up and down, "Yes that would be fine."

Great, I'm gonna get a new seat! There is a whole row of empty seats at the back of the plane, so I grab my stuff and plop down in one of those. I lie across three seats thinking maybe if there is a God, I will be able to sleep through some of this flight. Ten minutes after I sit down in my new seat the stewardess comes by to tell me, "You cannot sit in these seats sir."

"Well, why? I thought you said I could change seats. These are all empty."

"These are business class seats, you have only paid for coach."

I'm thinking bitch, you fuckers put me in half a seat for

a ten hour flight, fucked up my back, and now you wont let me have an empty seat nobody is sitting in anyways. But of course I'm cordial. "Oh, I'm sorry. I didn't realize. I'll move to another seat." So I find another empty seat, they all look the fucking same to me.

Stewardess again, "Sir, I told you you cannot sit in these seats. You need to move."

"Oh I'm sorry they all look the same, where can I sit?"

"In the seats up there." She points towards the front of the plane.

I was hoping maybe she would give me a hand at this point. All the seats further up in the plane are occupied in a way that I will have to sit next to another person to have a new seat. Which means I am going to have to ask some French Canadian motherfucker, in English, if it would be alright for me to sit next to them. Quebecois don't like to be spoken to in English, especially not by an unshaven, dirty, drunk American scum-bag.

So I'm wandering the plane looking for someone who seems nice and maybe wouldn't mind sitting next to a piece of shit such as myself for the next seven or eight hours. The plane has three seats on each side, and four in the middle. It's one of those. I walk up and down the isle a few times and decide on a woman who is roughly my age. She's in one of the middle seat sections on one end of the four, and a man is on the other end. There are two seats between them.

"Excuse me miss, I was wondering if it would be alright if I sat in that seat next to you? You see I have a situation with my current seat. There is not a lot of room in it, and my back is starting to hurt, I-"

201

"Of course. Here, you can just take my seat, and I will move over and sit next to my husband." Maybe there is a God. Thank you Jesus. I go, once again, to retrieve my things and move into my new home on the plane.

I return. The two people are still in their same seats. The woman hasn't moved. Her husband looks up at me, "I'm sorry you're not going to be able to sit in my wife's seat. I spilled a drink on the seat next to me. She can't sit here."

I'm starting to panic, "Um, there has to be something we can-"

"She can't sit here, I just told you. You wouldn't want my wife to have to sit in a wet seat now would you?"

Wife says, "Oh it's fine I can-"

"No, he's going to have to find somewhere else to sit, it's that simple."

OK there is no fucking God, but there is logic and reason. Something even these smurf talking fuck-balls can understand. I say, "Look, you know how at the beginning of every flight they explain how your seat cushion can be used as a flotation device? They're just velcroed down. So all you have to do is pull up the cushion next to you, swap it with the one next to your wife. Then she can sit next you, I can have her seat, and the dead seat will be next to me." He has a shit fit. Starts cursing in his retard French while throwing his hands in the air and flailing around. He's just making a fucking scene is what he's doing, it's ridiculous.

My apologies to any Quebecois reading this, (Yeah, the three or four of you out there.) but your French sounds like it's being spoken by a retarded leprechaun with a lisp.

I'm not claiming to have a super trained ear or anything in these matters, but at this point I've spent thirty or so days in real France, and y'alls shit is all fucked up. And I know, I use the word dude a lot. I've had to go back through this book several times to take out some of the fucks, shits, and dudes in it. If I didn't, that would be fifty percent of the content. You see my vocabulary is so limited that those are just my go-tos when it comes to nouns, verbs, and adjectives. I really don't have much else, therefore I tend to over use them. So don't take it too hard, all of us in North America seem a little dumb and low class compared to our European counterparts.

Hissy-fit eventually pulls up the cushions, like I begged him to, and his wife scoots over to sit next to him. Ah, I finally have a reasonable seat. After I'm seated I turn to her and say, "Thank you so much, you really saved me."

Wife, like a bitch, "You're welcome."

Now I'm not psychic or anything, and I didn't get to see this couple's tickets, but I'm gonna guess 99 out of 100 times when a married couple buys plane tickets, they don't buy them two seats apart. And if they could afford to buy the whole fucking row, they wouldn't be sitting in coach with a shit-bag like me.

For the next seven or so hours of the flight, husband and wife proceed to talk shit about me openly. You know, so I can hear it.

Husband, "Why the hell did you tell him he could have your seat?"

Wife, "I don't know, he just smelled so bad and I took pity on him I guess."

Husband, "He's getting up to piss again. Wow."

Wife, "Look he's drinking another beer, look at him go."

Husband, "Americans......"

I finally get back to America and go directly to my drug dealer's house to buy $80 worth of Xanax. I finally sleep and detox myself. I'm back to human form in a few short days. Jess takes me back sometime that summer, things are going well. Well actually they aren't because I keep falling off the wagon.

I get out-patient detoxed by my doctor for the second time in June of 2017 and I'm weaned off the benzos too quick. I have my second seizure on the summer solstice. This time I fall on Jess's hardwood floor and dislocate my right shoulder, one of the most painful things I've ever experienced. They have to knock me out at the hospital to pop it back in. That shit hurt for a whole year, still does if it gets tweaked.

In December I leave Jess for a Canadian girl named Karmin. She plays bass in a band I record. This is the second time I've left Jess for another woman. This is because I am a womanizer and a drunk.

In late February of 2018 I go to England to do some gigs. I don't think I'd had a drink in a month or so when I got on the plane, but on the plane I started again, just so I could sleep. That's what I tell myself, "You're just drinking to knock yourself out for this flight. When you get to England you're not gonna drink anymore." I brought a little Xanax of course, took a pill on the plane, washed it down with five or six drinks, and slept about half the flight, which is a complete God send for me since I can never sleep on planes. I left Oakland in the afternoon and got to London in the afternoon. I take The Tube from Heathrow to Thomas' place. He booked the three shows I'm supposed to play. Nico and Hugo are coming across the English Channel from Normandy to be my backing band. I'm doin' this shit in style. An American with a French backing band in London. This is great.

I meet Thomas for the first time in person, and of course, first thing he says to me is, "Well, you want to go down to the pub for a pint?" How's he supposed to know that this is a really bad fucking idea?

I say, "Why don't we just go to the store and get something?" I'm a drunk, but I'm also thrifty, and London is expensive. Plus I know you can drink anywhere and everywhere in England, I love this country.

We go to a liquor store. Thomas gets a couple pints of Guinness and I get a half pint of vodka. We walk around an ancient cemetery and get to know each other. Thomas made me a pair of shoes around five years prior to this. I'd done an interview somewhere along the way where I was asked about the white bucks I always wore. I told the interviewer that the shoes had been retired because they were so tattered after a decade of constant wear that no one would resole them. I always wore those shoes, they were famous. Well, if you really stretch the meaning of famous.

I played a festival in Chicago once at *The Empty Bottle*. We get to the venue after a long drive and I have to take a shit. I go straight for the men's room. The stall doesn't come anywhere near meeting the floor. It's of course a disgusting bar toilet that's all fucked up. So I'm in there doing my business, the venue is pretty full. Some kid comes into the crapper and sees my shoes under the stall. "Greg, is that Greg Ashley?" He opens the door to the bathroom back up and announces to the whole club, "Hey everybody, Greg Ashley's in here takin' a shit!"

"I've finally made it," I think to myself.

Anyways, Thomas read the interview and sent me a message saying, "Take a picture of the shoes and make a tracing of your feet. Send that to me and I'll make you a new pair of shoes." He did, and they're great. I still wear them. I wore them to England on this trip.

So no gig this first night, and we take it pretty easy, I think. Nico and Hugo show up the next morning. They've taken a boat across the channel overnight. We pile into a van with Thomas' band, *Mass Datura* and head to Leeds. We play with no practice, everything goes great of course, Nico and Hugo a pros. We all get drunk that night. It's so good to be with my French pals again. Next night is London. We kill it again, I see a whole mess of people I haven't seen since the last time I was in London, 13 years prior to this. We all get smashed.

OK, now I've crossed the threshold. I wake up the next day and have a couple to kill my hangover. This is the last gig of the trip. We drive to Nottingham, I drink vodka the whole way. Nico and Hugo look at me when we get to town and tell Thomas we're not playing. They know me, they've been through this bullshit before. Now it doesn't really matter that we don't play because no one shows up for this show anyways, but I still feel like an asshole for doing this to Nico and Hugo yet again. They go back to France the next day and I have three days to kill in London with nothing to do. Why have I done this shit again? My computer charger broke the day before, so now I feel super isolated. I have no contact with America. I start to drink all day everyday, just trying to sleep through the rest of my trip. I'm depressed and the weather is gloomy as fuck.

One day I go to the liquor store, buy my vodka, drink it on the street, and decide I'll get some lunch at a fast food place. I wake up in an ambulance. The paramedics tell me I fell down in the restaurant and hit my head. They put me through an MRI. I never get the results because I just leave the hospital once I'm sober enough to escape.

I find my way back to Thomas'. He pretty much tells me I should find another place to crash for the rest of my trip. His flat mates are not that excited about having me around anymore, and now I have a black eye. I've also missed my flight. I lost track of the days in my drunken stupor. Somehow I get a hold of my sister to help me. She buys me another flight home for the next day.

Luckily I have another French pal who's living in London at the time, Matthieu. He steps in to take care of me for what is supposed to be my last day in England. I crash at an *Air B & B* he's gotten. He takes me to the airport the next day. We part ways.

For some reason I can't find my gate, maybe because I'm fucking shit-faced again. I end up collapsing in the terminal, crying like a pathetic baby. I see more paramedics, they come to the conclusion that I'm drunk. Somehow Matthieu is there again with a representative from *Virgin Atlantic Airlines*. The guy from the airline proposes a deal, "Here is a voucher for food, another plane ticket for tomorrow, a bus pass, and a free hotel room for the night." I had incorrectly told him that I had no money in the world. He goes on, "You can have all of this under the condition that you do not drink anymore today. Take the bus to the hotel. I will inform the staff that you are not to be served alcohol of any sort. The same goes for the flight." At this point these people just want to get me the fuck out of their country, and this is a very, very good deal, except for the fact that not drinking is not an option for me at this point, but of course I take the deal. What the fuck else am I gonna do?

Matthieu comes to the hotel with me. He's been in contact with my sister and he's going to continue taking care of me until I get on that plane. He's an angel this man. Luckily the bartender at the hotel didn't get the memo so I get enough drinks in me to pass out. Next day, back to Heathrow. Matthieu and I part ways again. Another person I could never repay for their service as a friend. I'm a lucky bastard. This time I make my flight. I have a few in the terminal before boarding, just enough to stay well.

Luckily they don't get the memo on the flight either, until they do. Stewardess comes around for the first round of drinks. There's a group of British soccer bros, that are going to a tech conference, seated across the isle from me. One of them orders a double gin and tonic. Stewardess asks me what I would like. I reply, "Same as him, double gin and tonic." I get my drink and slam it.

About five minutes later the head stewardess of the plane comes by and says to me, "We have just gotten word that we are not to serve you any alcohol on this flight. Now you've had that one, and that is all fine and well, but I've informed the staff not to serve you anymore. We are not going to have a problem now are we?"

"No, of course not. I'm sorry." Yeah we're going to have a fucking problem. This is an eleven hour flight. I can't go that long without a drink.

So I sit there for the next six hours watching these douche bags get wasted, talking about soccer and internet bullshit. All the while I'm shaking and sweating with my black eye, having a panic attack. When will the seizure hit? If I don't get some more booze in me soon they're gonna have to land this bird in fucking Greenland or Canada or something. Finally I can't take it anymore. I get up and head for the back of the plane. I find the head stewardess. "Look I know what they told you, but if I don't have a drink soon, I'll have a seizure. I've had them before. I'm not drinking to get drunk and party, I just don't want to have a seizure. I'm begging you." She gives in and serves me a double. Partly out of mercy and party, I'm assuming, because she realizes that if I do have a seizure, they will have to land the plane. She serves me a couple more over the course of the flight, God bless her soul.

We land at SFO and I go through customs. They actually stop me and search my bag. I've never had this happen before, even coming back from Mexico. They probably search me because I'm shaking and sweating and I have a black eye. I look suspicious as fuck.

I get on BART, head back to Oakland. Halfway there, I again come to the conclusion that I'm not gonna make it. I get off at 24th and Mission and buy a pint of vodka. I drink it while waiting for the next train. I finally get back to Oakland and walk to Roadhouse's place. Him and Sofia greet me with a twelve pack of Natural Light and another pint of vodka. *Taka*, they know I have refined tastes. Ah, finally home with the best of friends. My parents call Roadhouse, I tell him to lie and say I'm sleeping. They have flown in from Texas and my sister has flown in from DC. They are all coming to figure out what to do with me.

The next day I meet up with them. I have to keep drinking to stay well. My sister has the job of supplying me with booze since I'm flat broke. I need detox. I go to The Ballerina, she doesn't wanna do it because she thinks it's too dangerous. She wants me to go to a hospital. My parents want me to go to rehab. I want the detox, but not the rehab. I keep drinking, we keep arguing. We're all at the church together, me and my family, and I see an opportunity to do something special. Something very, very special. I say, "OK, I'll go to rehab......... if you get high with me mom." Mom agrees, she's 76 years old and never gotten stoned. She confiscated my pipe in high school and gave it to the fucking *DARE* program. My parents took my bong when I was 16. They, for some reason, kept it in their closet till I was 18 and then threw it away right before I moved out. They knew I was gonna demand that shit back. And now my mom is gonna smoke with me, this is gonna be great! And it was..........

I pull out my pipe and take a hit. I blow the smoke into my mother's mouth. I do this three or four times. My mom has never smoked anything in her life, so this is how it has to be done. We get baked and listen to free jazz into the night, dancing and just having a ball. I've never had this much fun with my mom before. My sister and dad go back to their motel in Berkeley, mom sleeps on the recliner in the church.

They can't get me into detox for another day, so what

can I do? Gotta keep drinkin'. This night I decide I will take my dad hostage. "Alright dad, you're gonna stay here with me tonight and tell me your life story because you never talk and I have no idea what you were up to all those years before I came along." Dad stays at the church with me. He talks, I drink beer. I remember absolutely nothing he tells me about his life because I'm fucking drunk. What a waste.

The next day I end up in the John Muir Hospital Detox Ward for the second time in my life. Everything goes smooth. They don't give me a junky for a roommate this time, so I can actually sleep. My last stay here I got my own room at first, then in the evening they roll in another bed and announce to me, "You're getting a roommate."

I say, "Great."

"No, it's going to be OK," the orderly says. "I think you guys are gonna get along just fine." A guy with full on sleeve tattoos is ushered into my room. He immediately passes out, sleeps for like twelve hours.

I'm thinking to myself, "Well, maybe she was right. I'm getting along just fine with this dude, all he does is sleep."

When he wakes, we get to talking. He says to me, "Man, I did something I shouldn't have done. Right before I came here I shot the rest of the dope I had in the bathroom at my mom's house. I'm starting to get sick." The next two days I can't sleep cuz homeboy is writhing around in his hospital bed screaming and crying and puking. They don't give heroin addicts Suboxone or Methadone here so they just have to tough it out. Why the fuck are you people putting junkies and alcoholics in the same room together? You know what's going to happen, this isn't your first rodeo. Keep the alchies with the alchies and the junkies separate. Alcohol withdrawals might be more dangerous, but kicking heroin without the help of meds looks to me like a living hell. I've seen people go through it, but never this up close and personal. Eventually he goes to another facility or something, and I actually get to sleep.

My room-mate during stay number two was a fellow alcoholic, so no bullshit. He's a guy in his mid fifties named Michael, who works in the service industry. I don't know if he was a bartender or a waiter or what, but he told me he had been to John Muir for detox like 20 times or something. We get along fine, he's a personable guy, and we both keep a pretty tidy room and are quiet. I stay for three or four days, can't remember. I get out and then it's off to rehab.

Rehab is fucked up. They check me in and have me fill out hours of paperwork. They make sure to get my parent's money that's for sure. Medical doesn't cover rehab. The place is in Berkeley. I can't stand Berkeley. The lady checking me in takes all my belongings. Phone, wallet, etc..... "You are going in there with a bunch of junkies and criminals," she tells me.

The part of the facility where they check you in is immaculate. New plush leather couches, hardwood floors, very clean. This is the part my family sees. The part up the hill, where I will be living for the next month, is a dump. It's staffed entirely by ex-drug addicts who have all been through the program here. They are inconsiderate, rude, and short with all the inmates, because we are still drug addicted pieces shit and they are now cured and therefore better than us.

The first night they put me in a room with two other guys. They give me my sleeping pill and I'm off to bed. My bunkmates are an obese Mexican guy and an old white dude. I fall asleep pretty quick, but then am woken in the night by the Mexican. He not only has night terrors, but sleep apnea to boot. He's left his lamp on, pointed directly at my bed, so when he wakes me up wailing and moaning, I come to with the image of a large creature, back lit, with it's head in it's hands. Fucking freaks me out. He's up and down all night. When he's not moaning he's snoring, real fucking loud too. Gasping for breath over and over. On top of this an orderly comes in every hour and shines a flashlight on every bed in the room.

So I got homeboy making all this racket and then some asshole opening the door and shining a light in my eyes every hour on the hour. There's no way I'm getting back to sleep. Finally around three or four in the morning when the orderly comes in with her flashlight I get up and tell her I can't sleep in this room. We're standing right next to the big guys bed.

"Can you hear that?" I ask her.

"What, he's new, that's normal."

"No, he's not. He's not new, I'm the new guy. I'm new."

"Well what do you want me to do?"

"Well I need another room. I can't sleep in here, this is crazy."

Orderly is some wigger chick, total bitch. "I can't do nothin' for you, I'm sorry."

"There has to be another room I can sleep in, do you hear how loud that is?" We argue for around five minutes, finally she caves and gives me another room. There is plenty of empty rooms in this place actually.

Then it's on to arguing with this bitch about my sleep meds. "I need another sleeping pill, my prescription says on it, I can take one and then another if needed in the night." We go to the pill locker. Apparently this stupid bitch can't read or something. I have to point out the text on the bottle. "See, take 1-2 tablets orally at bedtime as needed. I've had my one, now I need my two." Dumb cunt finally gives me my pill and then I get in maybe two or three more hours of sleep.

The food in this place is just the lowest quality imaginable and so unhealthy. It reminds me of the cafeteria food I was served in elementary school in Texas. It's the cheapest, lowest quality, greasy old slop you've ever seen, and this is Berkeley. A supposed bastion of the healthy and fresh food movement. The fruit they have is obviously shit that has been donated from people's yards. I complain to my counselor, she tells me, "Well, there's a salad bar." This is like the salad bar at *Wendy's* in the 90's. The two choices of dressing are ranch and honey mustard. Great, real healthy.

So the food sucks, but they give me my own room for night two, which would be great except for the fact that it hasn't been cleaned in months. There's a thick layer of dust covering everything in the room, even the blankets. I don't complain though, anything is gonna be better than bunking with those guys from last night.

I try to sleep in that room that evening. My sinuses

close up from all the dust. It's the beginning of March and it's cold and rainy out, but I have to sleep with the window open and the fan on, or else I can't breath. I sleep in all my clothes with my coat on. That stupid bitch with the flashlight comes in and wakes me up every hour. Imagine you are sleeping peacefully in your freezing cold bed. You are woken by the sound of your bedroom door being opened. You jump out of bed, startled that there is an intruder in your home. A light is being shined in your eyes. Nevermind, no intruder here, it's just some wigger chick with an IQ of 70. Totally normal, just go back to bed. I never got used to it. It always freaked me the fuck out.

This place was totally set up like jail. The phones were pay phones. They were locked up the majority of the day. They told me I would need a phone card to contact the outside world. The other inmates showed me the trick to the phones. You have to get your hands on fifty cents first. You're not allowed any money in there, so that's a little bit of a challenge in itself. You give everybody on the outside you might wanna contact the numbers to the two pay phones. You tell them if they see either one of those numbers on their caller ID it's you. You put your change in, dial a number, and let the phone ring three times, then you hang up, get your two quarters back and hope whoever you were trying to reach calls you back.

It wasn't all bad though, I did do Yoga for the first time there. I loved it, felt so good afterward. We did some meditation too. That was OK, but mostly the "classes" were a fucking joke. On day two this college kid passes out on the couch in the TV room and nobody can wake him up. The staff freaks and calls an ambulance. We are ushered into our "stress management class", which consists of sitting in the dark, looking at a flat screen TV with a video of computer animated fish swimming around on it. Ambient guitar music plays in the background. What else is in the background? That poor kid being drug off by the paramedics kicking and screaming. "AH, YOU'RE HURTING ME! I WAS JUST SLEEPING! OWW, MY ARM, YOU'RE HURTING MY ARM. AHHHH!!!!!" Well that shit really lowered my fucking stress levels. Thank God for those fish. Maybe there's an app I can get for my Obama-phone. Every time I'm feeling a little edgy I'll just look down at the fishies. Woo!

The head mistress enters the room. "So you might have heard that little scuffle....." Yeah bitch, it was right outside the window, we all heard that shit. I'm going deaf, but I ain't there yet. "So Charlie is being taken to the hospital. We think he might have taken something."

Now I had had a conversation with this kid earlier. He was only a couple days away from completing his time in rehab. Charlie had been going to Chico State and was a month away from getting his undergrad degree when he fell out of his chair in class. You see he'd been addicted to opiates and benzos since he was a teenager. He had a football injury when he was 16, and of course his doctor prescribes him Oxycontin for the pain. The chronic pain. He was up to a pretty heroic dose by the time he graduated high school. He starts to sell some of his pills to make money. He goes off to college, has a nice little drug dealing business going on the side. He does well in class, tells me he would write papers and take tests without even remember doing those things. He gets good grades.

Man fucking sign me up. Imagine going to work and not remembering work? All the terrible boredom, taking shit from your boss, small talk, doing mindless, menial crap for eight hours, five days a week just so you can collect your slave wage. All of this erased out of your brain like it never happened with a paycheck waiting at the end.

Anyways, he tells me he's going back to school to finish his undergrad when he gets out. Then he is going to become a doctor specializing in addiction. He didn't seem the least bit interested in using from what I could tell. He seemed highly motivated to get on with his life.

Head mistress again, "We don't know what Charlie might have brought in here so we are going to need a urine sample from everyone and we'll need to search your rooms." What a load of shit. We all piss in cups while they flip our rooms. Next day, surprise! Kid wasn't on drugs and nobody else was either.

I'm starting to get tired of this shit at this point. I'm tired of being searched, harassed in the night, talked down to by a bunch of shit-bags and fed crap. I get called into my counselor's office later, not for any reason in particular, she just wants to talk about my "recovery". I don't remember what load of shit she spewed at me, but somewhere in this conversation she tells me, "Tonight is friends and family night." I can have visitors. Wow I think, great. She even lets me use her phone. I call Lars and Eric. They both come that evening. Now this friends and family night shit was represented to me as, we all just get to hang out with our friends and family. I didn't know what was coming down the pipe when I invited my homies to this creepy ass loony bin.

My pals show up that evening and I show them around the place. My counselor sees us out back and freaks out, "They can't be back here, only in the front room." Yeah the front room that is clean and has new furniture? What, you don't want the general public to see this fucking shit-hole dump that is masquerading as a center for treatment and recovery?

So we go back out front. Then all us inmates with our friends and family are forced to watch a video from the 1980s about addiction. Afterwards a presentation is given with a bunch of testimonials from inmates who have drank the K*ool-aid* and been successfully reprogrammed. It was odd and a little spooky to say the least. Lots of these fuckers liked being in here. They had been institutionalized. For like half of them it was a free vacation from life. The place took *Kaiser* and other insurances. These people weren't paying for their stay, it was covered by their insurance, which they had through their jobs. Their jobs had sent them here to get clean. They were collecting workman's comp from their jobs. So they not only weren't paying, they were being paid to sit on their ass in this place with free room and board for a month. Many of them were trying to get more time. Fucking crazy. I think rehab should certainly be covered by insurance, but this place and these people were gaming the system for sure. The *New Bridge Foundation* was making a killing.

At the end of the presentations and all the bullshit, they give us ten minutes to hang with our visitors and then kick everyone out. I felt sorry for Eric and Lars, but I think they kind of enjoyed how strange the whole thing was. Once in a lifetime experience I suppose. Certainly for me, I'll never go back to a rehab. I left the next day.

I try to date Karmin long distance, but it doesn't really work. The two of us travel back and forth between Oakland and Vancouver to see each other. I have big plans to go up and spend August of 2018 with her. Then I get a DUI. Now I can't enter Canada for ten years, so that relationship is dead.

I continue to drink and smoke crack. I get robbed and beat up by some hood. My old girlfriend Lisa steps in and buys me a plane ticket to LA to stay with her while I get my shit together and let everything in my neighborhood calm down. I stay with Lisa for ten days. I detox by slowly weaning myself off of booze this time. I don't have any pills. I slowly drink less and less beer everyday until I'm down to nothing. Except now I can't sleep at night. I haven't been able to get an appointment with The Ballerina to get my RX for sleeping pills renewed, and I'm having trouble getting the clinic to renew the RX over the phone in the meantime. I'm trying to get them to send it down to LA.

I secretly buy a half pint of vodka the last two nights I'm there and slam it at bedtime. It's the only thing I can think of to do to get some sleep and stop my mind from running in circles.

I get back to Oakland and actually feel pretty good. The day after I return, I go to Roadhouse's for a shower and have a seizure on his porch. He rushes me to the emergency room at Summit Hospital, a place I will visit at least twice after that in 2018 for detox related things.

I guess after that I'm OK for a bit, but I still can't get in to see my doctor for my sleep meds. They keep pushing my appointment back, so I start drinking again. I don't know how long this lasts cuz I can't remember any of it, probably three weeks. That's usually the amount of time I booze before my life completely falls apart and all my friends start to give up on me.

This time I detox myself with Xanax. I wasn't about to go to the detox hospital covered by my Medical (Obama Care). I did that shit once and it was fucking scary. I remember I got dropped off there by my friend Sahar, the orderlies told her she couldn't come in. It was the detox for the county jail I'm pretty sure. Fucking looked like jail. The orderlies tell me to sit on this metal bench and they'll be with me in a minute.

An hour goes by with different insane, crazy motherfuckers coming through the waiting room, screaming and crying and shit. The receptionist is in a bullet proof room inside the waiting area. She deals with this Mexican dude for a while, then he goes into some other room. I continue to wait, there's nobody else in there now, but they don't call my name or acknowledge me in any way.

Finally I have to take a piss, so I go up to the counter and very politely, of course, ask if she would like to take my bag while I use the restroom. She says, "You haven't been helped yet?"

"No, you told me to wait on the bench."

She point towards a hallway, "Bathroom's over there, we'll get you checked in when you come out."

So I walk in the direction that she pointed, and all

there is there, is the employee bathroom. I figure she's letting me use the employee bathroom. I walk down the hall and an orderly comes out and starts yelling at me, "You can't be back here! What the hell are you doing?"

"The lady at the desk told me this is where the bathroom is, I'm sorry." Mind you I'm totally fucking frazzled already from alcohol withdrawals. I have just been sitting on some bench for an hour shaking and sweating and having a panic attack.

The orderly directs me into a glass room that is like a long wide hallway. He says, "Bathroom's in the back, don't open the door back there or the alarm will go off." So I walk down this wide dimly lit hallway. There are guys on pads on the floor all down the hall shaking and crying, fucking going through withdrawals. The toilet is behind a shower curtain at the back of the room. I piss, come back out front, get my shit and get the fuck out of there. I Call my friend to pick me back up.

So no Cherry Hill Detox Center for me, fuck that place. I do the things I know I need to do to get through this again. I take Xanax for a week, slowly tapering down the dosage. What I did not take into consideration here was the fact that while I had gotten down to no Xanax during the day, I was still taking a milligram every night to sleep cuz I still haven't been able to see my doctor.

Finally my appointment comes up and they don't cancel it like they did the last two. I see The Ballerina, tell her what is going on and she writes me a script for Ambien or Seroquel or whatever the fuck I'm taking at this point.

That night I take regular sleeping pills instead of Xanax, not thinking about the fact that my body has remained dependent on benzos because I've been taking them every night. I had put them in a category in my mind that made them sleeping pills instead of benzos.

The next day I go to Arlo's to shower and use his computer. I am there till around 3pm I suppose. I ride my bike home. I'm riding down the middle path of Mandela Parkway and I black out. I come to wandering the streets of West Oakland bleeding out of my face like a zombie. People are coming up to me and asking me if I'm alright. Do I look alright motherfucker? I'm trying to figure out what's going on and find Arlo's house.

At some point Sean from Jess's house finds me. He was walking his dog down Mandela and found my bike next to a pool of blood. Then Arlo and Thatcher show up. We go back to Arlo's, I don't feel like going to the hospital today. They wanna take me to the emergency room but I'm not having it. I broke my other front tooth in half. I had a deep scrape across my face from my forehead, down my nose and onto my chin. The tops of my hands are cut up too. I must have had a seizure while I was riding my bike and just collapsed face first onto the cement.

So that's a bitch and now I need to make another appointment with my doctor. Soonest I can see her is in like a month, so I just keep working and going to my court required AA and paying my lawyer and going to court, and on and on and on.

I start drinking again in there, go to Summit Hospital, get them to write me a script for detox pills. I detox, then finally get to see my doctor, and finally get the right medications for everything. Lots of sleep aids and anti seizure pills. I stop drinking, I start drinking. Over and over and over again, but this is it. It's 2019 now and I'm through with this shit. I want to live. And now I'm going to finish this book, and this part of my life.

-THE END-

So this books not supposed to be some kind of memoir or anything. It's just a bunch of fucked up stories from my life that I figured somebody else could have a chuckle, or a cringe at. They're anecdotes, for the most part, I told a million times at the bar in my re-run of an existence. And that's just how it is when you're an alcoholic. You do the same shit over and over and you always get to the same place. You repeat the same mistakes again and again. You never learn. You do things like:

1. Get in stupid arguments and say dumb shit.
2. Stay up late doing nothing and listening to the same records you've heard a million times before.
3. Smoke crack. Well maybe you smoke crack anyways, that shit's fun every once in a while. Never mind, never smoke crack. It's a bad fucking idea. I smoked a shit load of crack since I wrote this, and nothing good came of it.
4. Lose job after job after job. Most jobs it's OK cuz you didn't want them in the first place, you just had to take them to survive, but I've lost a couple that I actually wanted. A couple........
5. Drive fucked up.
6. Fuck a person you do not actually like.
7. Piss yourself.
8. Have a seizure.
9. Be in general a terrible person, possibly resembling a sociopath. (See The Dutchess and The Duke tour diary.
10. Put everyone in the world that you love through the nightmare of watching someone they love step into the void over and over again.

And you can see how I got to this place in the pages of some of these stories. Sure everybody parties in high school. Maybe not like me and my friends, but you get fucked up some, at least most people do. But if when you leave high school, and after a few years, you become say, I don't know, a musician, and your job is to play the same songs over and over again, night after night, in some dingy bar that is feeding you free booze, you develop a little stronger thirst than the average person.

I remember coming home from the first big *Gris Gris* tour and not knowing what to do with myself but go to the bar that night. I chose to hang out at the fucking *Stork Club* of all places. It had become routine. Some people can handle it, but I can't. Fucking sucks. And like I said before, I might come off as an asshole that's talking shit in this book. That's because I am an asshole that's talking shit, but I don't wanna be that way anymore.

I love all these people, all the characters that have shaped me as a person over the years. And all these fuckers are definitely characters, real characters. I wouldn't be writing about them if they weren't. I also don't want people reading this to see these characters, including myself, as existing in suspended animation or something. These are stories from a specific time and place in the past written from the perspective of that time and place. They are in no way supposed to be a comprehensive representation of who these people are today or even were back then. I know I've gotten some places, times and people wrong here and there in unimportant places (I've changed some names where I thought it would be prudent) but I don't care, it doesn't matter. These are just anecdotes, and this is generally how

I remember some of it. Who knows if any of this even happened. Every time you have a memory they say you don't actually remember it, you just re-create it, sometimes very differently from how it really happened.